PIE IT FORWARD

PIE it FORWARD

PIES, TARTS, TORTES, GALETTES

& other

PASTRIES REINVENTED

GESINE BULLOCK-PRADO

STEWART, TABORI & CHANG   NEW YORK

Published in 2012 by Stewart, Tabori & Chang
An imprint of ABRAMS

Library of Congress Cataloging-in-Publication Data:

Bullock-Prado, Gesine.
Pie it forward : pies, tarts, tortes, galettes, and other pastries
reinvented / Gesine Bullock-Prado ; photography by Tina Rupp.
p. cm.
Includes index.
ISBN 978-1-58479-963-4
1. Pies. 2. Pastry. I. Title.
TX773.B887 2012
641.86'52—dc23
2011039855

Editor: Natalie Kaire
Designer: Alissa Faden
Production Manager: Tina Cameron
Prop Stylist: Deborah Williams

The text of this book was composed in Archer, Gotham, Walbaum, and Chalet.

Printed and bound in U.S.A.

10 9 8 7 6 5 4 3 2 1

Stewart, Tabori & Chang books are available at special discounts when purchased
in quantity for premiums and promotions as well as fundraising or educational use.
Special editions can also be created to specification. For details, contact
specialsales@abramsbooks.com or the address below.

THE ART OF BOOKS SINCE 1949
115 West 18th Street
New York, NY 10011
www.abramsbooks.com

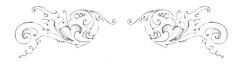

For my schatzi, Raymo.

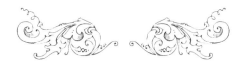

CONTENTS

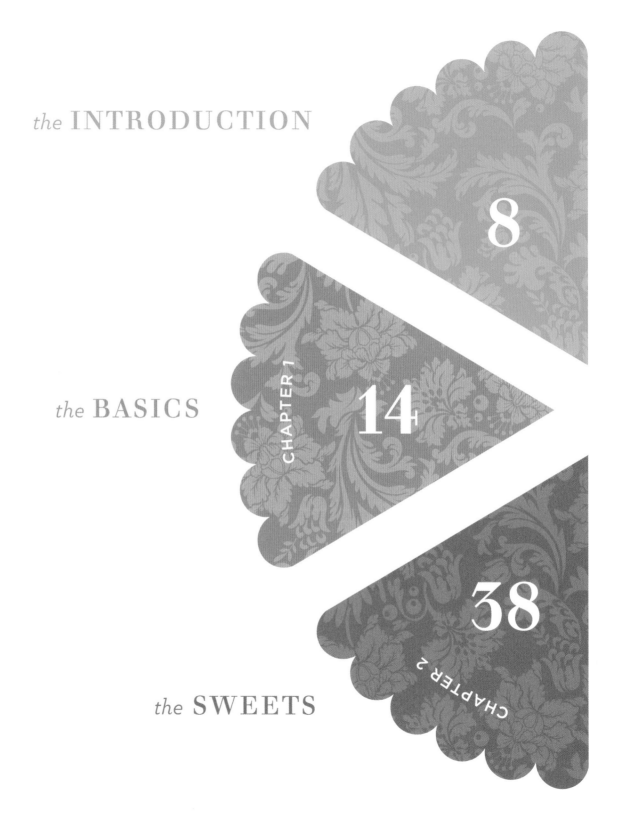

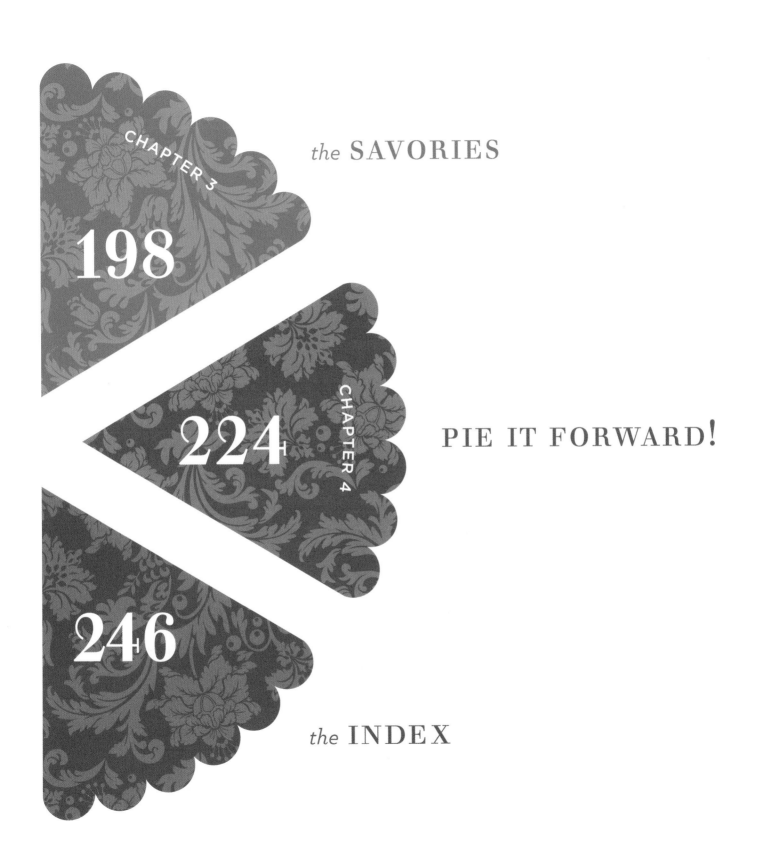

the INTRODUCTION

You think you know pie: the double crusts, the lattices, the crumbles, and the pots. But what do you REALLY know about it? Can you honestly say that in your relationship with these flaky and tender-crusted vessels of deliciousness you've bothered to ask about pie's past, its adventures in history, and its development from a thick-walled, inedibly crusted caloric delivery system to a coveted homespun delicacy? I thought not. As the resident pie expert and official member of the High Order of the Keepers of the Crust, I have orchestrated this introduction:

READER, MEET PIE. PIE, MEET READER.

READER: So how old are you, really?

PIE: Older than most sparkly vampires—thousands of years old. On your next visit to Egypt, you may spot my image etched onto the walls of pyramids.

As a matter of fact, Pharaoh Ramses II, recognized as supreme leader AND a pie fan, was so besotted with the crusty stuff that his tomb bears images of galettes. The Greeks and Romans used pastry to encase savory fillings, making them more portable and giving sailors some culinary variety on long sea journeys. The first hit cookbook, written by Apicius, has any number of recipes devoted to pastry cases filled with a wondrous assortment of goodies, from honey-soaked almonds to minced meats. The most popular pie of the day (that day being around the start of the fifth century) had the unfortunate moniker of Placenta. Thankfully, it wasn't an afterbirth potpie, but an ancient variation on our beloved cheesecake. So remember next time you're eating a cheesecake, you're really eating the oldest known pie.

READER: How'd you get that catchy name?

PIE: It's been so many years I don't quite remember anymore, but some say I was named after the magpie, a bird that has an affinity for collecting bits of disparate pieces of junk, at which I take umbrage. Sure, early "humble pies" once consisted of anything remotely edible shoved into a thick-walled flour crust and baked until any vestige of taste was eradicated, so I can see how I could once have been equated with a clinically insane feathered hoarder, but we've come so far since then.

READER: What's so easy about "easy as pie"?

PIE: Who are you calling easy? I'm just not that kind of girl. Now, Cake, she's easy. Just put a bunch of ingredients in a bowl, and she's ready to do your bidding. I, on the other hand, take a little wooing. My crust needs attention, and my filling is an entirely separate undertaking from the delicious flaky vessel. What is easy about me is the eating. Back in the day, pies like delicious Cornish pasties were handheld affairs, small enough to carry in your pocket to the mines but hearty enough to nourish throughout the day. So while my preparation isn't necessarily easy, eating me can be.

READER: Is it true that crusts make the pie, and have crusts always been so darn tasty?

PIE: Yes and no. A pie just isn't a pie without the crust(s), this much is true. But don't get me started on what crusts used to be. First off, a crust very early on served as a vessel alone and wasn't exactly edible. It was thick walled, inches wide even, and was constructed from a flour-and-water paste not unlike Play-Doh . . . just not as tasty. Crusts had to be dense and damn hard to withstand hours, maybe days, of cooking. They needed to be sturdy because they were made for storage. Fittingly, those inedibly crusted pies with tops and bottoms were once called "coffyns," while those with just a bottom crust were named "traps." There were no pie dishes; the crust was the dish and probably tasted just as good as a hearty bite of Pyrex. Consider yourself lucky that some glorious baker thought to make the crust edible by adding a generous dose of fat.

READER: Four-and-twenty blackbirds? Singing? Really?

PIE: Think what you may, but yes, I've been known to house live songbirds in my day. What's more, minstrels used to hide in me and pop out to sing a ditty or two between the MANY courses of Henry Tudor's dinner parties. A naked lady jumping out of a cake is quaintly 1950s. Jumping out of a pie, however, is old-school 1480s.

When the birds weren't living, they were still displayed in all their whole, feathered glory; the carcass that had once encased the yummy contents of a pie would be draped over the pastry to identify and adorn it. King Henry VI's coronation was celebrated with peacock pie, and the English went on making these bird pies until Victorian times. They couldn't stop themselves from shoving all manner of songbirds into a piecrust (even when it was illegal to fell the sweet warblers). Thankfully, the tradition of "dead bird on pie" was eventually forsaken and, instead, porcelain birds were settled into the pie and allowed to peek out, creating both a form of pie identification and a vent for steam.

READER: Is apple pie really all that American?

PIE: Yes, of course. Berry pies, probably even more so. And don't get me started on pumpkin. Pies in the Old Country were most often savory. In the New World, industrious cooks plucked and picked what was immediately available and, like the good locavores they were, filled their pies with what was nearby, like indigenous berries and tree fruits. Thrifty Pilgrims used shallow pans lined with pastry as a vessel for baking local berries and a baking tradition took hold in the Americas, giving rise to a pantheon of splendid American beauties like apple pie, pecan pie, sour cherry pie, and the nonpie pies like Boston cream pie (likely named because locals used a pie plate to bake the cake layers).

And since provisions like flour were scarce, they had to "cut corners"—they literally made the pies round. That's where the phrase comes from! True story!

READER: Is a tart a pie?

PIE: Yes. So is a galette. Anything with a crust (that's not a cake) and with yummy fillings is pie in my book. While the traditionalists would maintain that the shape has to be just so, with the crust acting as a baked bowl for the fillings, I defy anyone to tell me that I can't get dressed up once in a while. I like to go "sleeveless" now and again, like when I wear a jazzy number called a "napoleon," with layers of pastry and creamy fillings galore. I know it may offend some, but there are days that I like to expose my assets. Other times, I like to wrap myself in finery, perhaps in a whirlwind of flaky crust, as in a strudel, or some days I prefer a little dark chocolate or jaunty joconde decoration. Why do cakes get all the attention? I can be as fancy or as casual as I please. I am Pie, hear me roar. Or more precisely, YOU can make me roar. Now, get to it.

It's a conundrum I can't understand. Someone's hankering for pie; you can see the pie-longing in their eyes. They want a delicious flaky crust, something with buttery overtones. They want fresh fruit—not a vague whisper of berry in a buttercream, but overt chunks of apple, discernible bites of berry. But it's just not done. You don't serve pie at special events like fiftieth birthdays, dinner parties, silver anniversaries, or, God forbid, at a wedding. To which I reply, "Bullpuckies."

At my shop, Gesine Confectionary, Friday was "Pie Day." The pastry case paid homage to all things pie and, because I am of both European and American extraction, my view on what constitutes "pie" is expansive. On any given Friday, you could find double-crust caramel apple pie, brown butter wild blueberry pie, latticed sour cherry pie and blackberry crumble pie, strawberry-rhubarb pie, lemon meringue pie, Key lime custard pie, tiramisu tart, mango curd meringue pie, apricot tarte tatin, German apfel strudel, free-form coconut-caramel-ganache tarts, chicken potpie, Bavarian-inspired calzone, ham-and-cheese turnovers, Boston cream pie, quiche, free-form pear galette, frangipane pithivier, chocolate cream pie, strawberry cream pie, apricot-rhubarb tart, pecan tart, pumpkin mousse pie, macaron tart . . .

And the great thing? Whether you bought them in individual sizes straight from the case (see page 55) or ordered them large, I always took pains to make them beautiful. Beautiful enough for a birthday and, if you wanted them that way, spectacular enough for a wedding.

While pie may have a fixed definition in the average American lexicon to only include those pastries Mrs. Cleaver might have cooling on her windowsill on any given day, on Elm Street we traveled back as far as pie history might take us.

Pastry and filling made a diverse and delicious marriage throughout Europe, giving rise to galettes, pizza pies, quiche, napoleons, strudels, and a rainbow of tortes and tarts. These all found their way into my pastry case.

I'd like to share my journey with you, so that you may explore pie in all its glory, elevate it with your very own elegance, and share it with the people you love—so that you may pie it forward.

A FEW THINGS YOU'LL NEED TO MAKE PIE LIFE EASIER

Nimble fingers: The number-one priority for great pie making. If you are without a food processor, possessing a good set of baker's hands will do the trick. Sadly, you can't refrigerate your fingers like you can butter and flour, so if your digits tend toward the warm, avoid manhandling the dough. If you're like me and suffer from poor circulation that results in icy fingers, dive in! Otherwise, the hot-fingered without a food processor should invest in a handheld pastry blender.

Food processor: Many of my pie doughs begin in the food processor. The sharp blades of the machine make blending the dough quick stuff, which reduces the amount of time you spend mixing and potentially overworking the gluten. Overworking leads to tough and rubbery dough—but the blitz action of this machine leaves you with tenderness instead. Using one also allows you to freeze your fats prior to adding them to the flour, which is impossible when blending with your tender fingers. And the processor comes in handy for fillings like frangipane or for pulverizing nuts and making fruit purées.

Electric mixer: While electric mixers are usually the stuff of cake and cookie making and not the standard in the pie world, they are pretty indispensable when preparing pastry creams, puff pastry, and pizza and strudel dough. When developing gluten is key to the process, give your muscles a break and let the machine sweat it out for you!

Rolling pin: My preference is a French rolling pin, one that tapers at the ends. But any sturdy pin, whether it's French, marble, or a wine bottle, is key to rolling out your lovely crusts.

Pie weights: When blind baking a pie or tart crust, weighing down the dough when it first starts baking is an essential step on the way to a beautiful finished product. You can use dried beans or uncooked rice as a weight, but I'm a huge fan of ceramic pie weights. First, unlike dried beans, they don't get smellier the more you bake them. Second, you can clean them easily. Third, their round shape is perfect for fitting into sharp corners (like when you're making a rectangular tart), so you can keep the shape of the crust uniform. I buy four packs of weights at a time: One pack alone usually isn't enough for a single shell. I also like to fill the entire shell, not just line the bottom. I do this to prevent the sides of the crust from slouching down, which can happen with delicate doughs. That requires extra weights, so you might as well have them on hand.

Tart forms, flan forms, Pyrex pie plates: Pies can take any number of shapes. They can be large or tiny. They can be made in glass pie plates or in metal tart forms. Unless you are a professional pastry chef, sometimes it's a mystery to home bakers what to use for certain tarts or pies. For instance, my favorite tool for making tarts is a flan ring. It's a bottomless, thin metal ring that might look useless to a home cook unfamiliar with its purpose. Actually, it's the standard form used in French bakeries for most tarts. But how the heck are you supposed to know that when the darn thing is called a FLAN ring and not a tart ring or a pie mold? I'll give you ideas, resources, and the right names for the different shapes my pies and tarts will take. Your pie world will open up. I promise.

www.pieitforwardcookbook.com: This is your resource for all things extra, like video demos of very cool techniques for making pie pops, strudel dough, and joconde décor sides, or wrapping a tall pie with chocolate transfer sheets.

CHAPTER

1

the
BASICS

Making a great crust is crucial to pie perfection, but not every pie is going to sing with the same crust recipe. Therefore, I'm giving you my entire lineup of crusts for every possible pie occasion up front, from puff pastry to pizza crust. On top of that, there are recipes for fillings that show up in any manner of combinations, so having them now will familiarize you with the recipes that should always have at your fingertips. Think of these recipes as a great foundation for the deliciousness that's to come.

THE CRUSTS

CRUST IS QUEEN IN THE PIE WORLD. If you can't muster together a beautiful crust, your creation isn't worth shoving into anyone's piehole, no matter how delicious the filling might be. You should also keep in mind that choosing the right type of crust to house your filling is as essential as how well you make the thing. For a double crust, you have to ask yourself whether you are willing to forsake a little bit of unruly buttery, flaky lusciousness for a modicum of control. You see, if you go with a quick puff for a double crust, you have to be ready for your handiwork (beautiful crimping and perfect lattice) to take on a life of its own, as quick puff tends to rise and grow in the heat of the oven according to its own whim. Choose the easy pie dough in all-butter or with a little shortening, and you have beautiful taste combined with aesthetic control.

If you opt to use a sweet crust with an even sweeter custard filling instead of selecting the less cloying simple tart crust, my dad would say you're "gilding the lily." In other words, you're smothering the essence and goodness of the tart. You must seek balance in pies, a gentle dance of flavor and texture. Having an arsenal of gorgeous pie and tart crusts at your fingertips will ensure that you get that balance right every time.

LET'S TALK ABOUT FAT.

There is no pie or tart crust worth shoving in your piehole without it. Usually the fat we're talking about is butter; that's my personal favorite. Butter, well handled, produces flaky, tender, and crispy crusts. To get specific and a little technical, I prefer to use unsalted European butter. European butter has a higher butterfat content and lower moisture than your run-of-the-mill grocery-store butter. This leads not only to elevated levels of flakiness and tenderness, but also to less shrinkage in the oven while baking, because there's less water to evaporate away.

However, butter is notoriously unruly when it hits the oven. Your perfectly crimped edges, when confronted with the full blast of pie-baking heat, can morph into flaky blobs or simply drop off into the cavern of your oven, left to smolder evermore on the bottom of your gas range.

This is where vegetable shortening comes in. It's incredibly stable at high temperatures, which means that a crust made with a percentage of shortening will hold its shape better, and its edges and cutouts will stay pristine while baking. It's also much cheaper than butter. That said, shortening leaves a telltale film in your mouth, which some find less than pleasant. So weigh your options and priorities when choosing all butter or part shortening.

In America, the long-lost and glorious pastry fat is leaf lard. It's made of the fat that surrounds a porker's kidneys and, when added to flour to make pastry, combines the best of butter's flaky and tender qualities with nuttiness and a soupçon of bacon goodness that's hard to beat. (The butter-to-leaf-lard ratio has to be exact. I've found that adding more than 25 percent lard will produce a crust redolent of a pig roast instead of simply adding a hint of salty goodness.)

Unfortunately, leaf lard is terribly hard to come by in the United States these days, and often when you do get your hands on it, it's poorly processed—it tastes of pigpen instead of pork goodness when it bakes off. However, well-rendered lard is glorious. Prairie Pride Farm in Minnesota is a great online resource for it; otherwise, ask your butcher if he's got any.

Suet is another lovely option. It's the rendered fat of a cow's kidney and produces similarly tasty results when added to pastry. If you have the wherewithal to render your own fat, I highly recommend the effort. You'll not regret the gorgeous deliciousness it adds to your crust.

But there's nothing wrong with sticking to the easy-to-find options: butter and vegetable shortening.

HERE'S THE DEAL WITH FLOUR.

Different flours have different percentages of gluten, from cake flour, with the lowest, to bread flours, with the highest. But even though most brands offer a cake, an all-purpose, and a bread flour, the average flour mills won't guarantee consistent gluten percentages—they just aim for a range and call it a day. I'm not going to name any names, but they are the usual grocery suspects. When I hear the a baker lament, "I did everything exactly the same as always, but it all went to hell," I immediately ask, "What kind of flour do you use?" The truth is, you could have mixed your ingredients exactly as you did when you made that cake perfectly, only to have it come out rubbery and full of holes this time. Chances are, the gluten levels in the new bag of flour you just bought are higher.

As a rule, I use all-purpose flour in my piecrusts and tart doughs. Specifically, I use King Arthur, which is the only flour mill I know that guarantees exact gluten percentages in each of its flours. I work the flour as little or as much as I need, depending on the kind of crust I'm making. If I'm making a sweet dough or a butter crust, I use a food processor and work the fats into the dough with quick pulses so as not to overwork the glutens. If I'm working with a yeasted dough for a crust—like in *Zwetschgendatschi* or a pizza pie or a puff pastry—I mix the dough enough to increase gluten for protein structure and great mouthfeel.

A NOTE FROM THE SWEETIE PIE
Unsalted Butter

I've been asked over and over, "Why unsalted butter in your recipes? I *like* salted butter." And I always answer, "Because I say so!"

And then I take a deep breath, count to ten, eat a piece of pie, find my inner baker's calm, and actually answer the question like an adult.

First, salt is a preservative. Its use in products like butter is to extend shelf life. This means the salted butter in your grocer's cold case is very likely to be older than the unsalted butter. Fresher is better.

Second, just because salt is a preservative doesn't mean there isn't something about the butter that can't go a little off during that extra time it spends hanging around waiting for you to stroll down the refrigerated aisle and give it a second glance. That butter has a chance to pick up a few things, and what it ends up acquiring is what I like to call "butter funk," a smell and taste reminiscent of a communal dirty-laundry sack in a pro football locker room. I have an uncanny ability to identify any product made with salted butter that had lingering funk, and I'll have none of it in my own work.

Third, no one is going to tell me how much salt to put into my recipe. I'm making everything from scratch, so why would I want someone shoving salt willy-nilly into my glorious butter products? That's my job!

All-Butter Easy Pie Dough

THIS DOUGH IS TERRIBLY EASY TO MAKE, BUT IS STILL INCREDIBLY BUTTERY AND TASTY. You have two options: You can make it with all butter for full flakiness or add a little shortening to lend greater workability to the mix. Both are great options for double-crust pies.

Makes enough dough for 1 (9-inch/23-cm) double-crust pie

all-purpose flour, cold	2 cups	250 g
salt	1 teaspoon	6 g
sugar	1 tablespoon	11 g
unsalted butter, cut into small pieces and chilled in the freezer for 10 minutes	1 cup	225 g
ice water (Don't add the ice to the pie dough, just the water.)	½ cup	120 ml
lemon juice	1 teaspoon	5 ml

1. In the bowl of a food processor fitted with the blade attachment, pulse together the flour, salt, sugar, and butter until the mixture resembles cornmeal.

2. In a small bowl, stir together the ice water and the lemon juice. Slowly add the liquid to the flour mixture, pulsing, until the dough just comes together. Squeeze a small piece of dough between your thumb and index finger to make sure it holds its shape.

3. Turn the dough out onto a lightly floured surface and divide it in half. Gently turn over each piece of dough a few times so that any dry bits are incorporated. Form each piece into a loose disk, cover the dough with plastic wrap, and let it rest in the refrigerator for at least 20 minutes.

A NOTE FROM THE SWEETIE PIE
Blind Baking!

Blind baking simply means baking the piecrust before you add the filling. This usually means you are baking it completely because the filling doesn't require any more baking. Many cream pies, flan and panna cotta tarts, and pies filled with mousses and pastry cream have no-bake fillings that require the crust to be fully baked ahead of time.

But blind baking can also signify that you are just par-baking, which means you're partially baking the crust before adding a filling, at which point you'll bake the entire pie. This prevents the bottom crust from getting soggy. It's obviously something you usually only do with a single-crusted pie, since with a double-crusted pie you can only properly crimp together the top and bottom crusts around the edges when both pieces of the dough are raw—if you want a very clean double-crusted pie, that is. I blind bake double-crusted bottom crusts when I'm not feeling particularly precious about how perfectly the edges of the pie will come out or if the top crust is going to be made up of overlapping cutouts.

OPTIONS!

Option 1 Part-Butter/Part-Shortening Easy Pie Dough
Reduce the amount of chilled, unsalted butter to 12 tablespoons (170 g) and add 4 tablespoons (50 g) shortening, chilled in the freezer for 10 minutes.

Option 2 Easy Rustic Pie Dough
Cornmeal is a lovely addition to pie dough when you want to add a rustic feel to your dough. Replace ¼ cup (30 g) of the flour with ¼ cup (40 g) of finely ground cornmeal.

You've heard this a thousand times: Your pie dough ingredients must be bitterly frigid before proceeding. This is advice you must really take to heart. The rule of thumb in professional bakeries is that a pie or tart dough should never be warmer than 60°F (16°C).

First, no matter whether the fat you are using is butter, vegetable shortening, or lard, it must be ice-cold or the fat will be absorbed into the flour and create a tough crust. When it's all but frozen, the fat gets layered in between the flour, and its moisture is released in the heat of the oven, creating a flaky and tender crust.

Second, if your fat is cold but your flour, water, and work surfaces are warm, what's the point of having gone through all the trouble of cooling the fat in the first place? Keeping the fat suspended and whole within the dough is crucial to tender and flaky, so it only follows that if the rest of the elements are cold too, then you'll fare better at keeping your butter in the perfect state of suspended animation until it's time to bake! So I store my flour in the refrigerator when I'm making pie dough.

Third, ice water is the standard liquid used in pie and tart crusts, but that doesn't mean you actually pour the ice into the mix—just the ice-cold water. I make a large pitcher of ice water a half hour ahead of time, place it in the fridge, and, when I'm ready, pour the icy-cold water into my measuring cup and proceed with my crust. Add only enough cold water to hydrate and moisten the dough, but never so much that it gets soggy. Too little liquid, however, will lead to a crumbly and unworkable dough. Depending on the relative moisture during any given day, you'll notice that you'll need more or less water for your dough to come together. So always add water *slowly*, not all at once, to allow for atmospheric differences.

Fourth, if you are using a food processor to make dough, you can first cube your fats into small pieces and then freeze them completely. The blades make easy work of cutting through the stuff, and you'll be ahead of the curve in the cold-dough game. On the other hand, if you don't have a food processor, you can still freeze your fat (this actually works best with butter), then shred it into your dough with a box grater, using the large holes.

Fifth, roll your dough out onto a cool work surface. Marble is often used because it's naturally cold to the touch. It's easy to forget, when you're busy in the kitchen, that you've just moved a hot sheet pan from your usual rolling area, leaving what should be your cool pastry space hot as hell. So when working on pies and tarts, keep a designated work area "roped off" and cool for exclusive pastry use. Keep it free from all other kitchen clutter and hot pots and sheet pans.

Sixth, let your dough rest in the fridge or freezer for at least twenty to thirty minutes after you've first mixed it and then again after rolling it into a round to line a pie or tart pan. Manipulating and rolling dough works the gluten in the flour, which is the protein in wheat that gives it elasticity. The more you work a dough with flour, the more elastic and rubbery it becomes. That's why we knead bread dough—to develop the gluten well and produce that gorgeous bready texture. Conversely, that's why you *don't* knead pie dough: We don't want chewy or tough, we want tender and flaky. But any amount of manipulation of flour gets the protein worked up and tense. If you don't allow your dough to rest for twenty to thirty minutes before using it, you'll notice that as you're trying to make an ordinary 11-inch (28-cm) round of dough for a 9-inch (23-cm) pie plate, the dough won't maintain its shape or size and will shrink back. That's because it needs some alone time, to rest and relax all of those *verklempt* proteins. Likewise, if you don't allow a rolled dough a decent amount of rest before baking, it will shrink in the oven.

Bottom line: The trick to making great pie and tart dough is to keep it cool and relaxed.

Simple Tart Dough

THIS IS MY GO-TO DOUGH FOR ANYTHING THAT NEEDS SIMPLICITY AND TEXTURE. It is akin to the French classic *pâte brisée*, but with so much more flavor (in my not-so-humble opinion). The inclusion of sweetened condensed milk might have you thinking that this is a sweet dough, but it's not. Instead, the milk adds an underlying caramel richness without making a sweet crust.

Makes 2½ pounds (1.2 kg) dough, enough for 3 to 4 (8- to 9-inch/20- to 23-cm) tarts or 12 to 16 mini tarts

all-purpose flour, cold	4 cups	500 g
unsalted butter, cut into small pieces and chilled	2 cups	480 g
salt	1 teaspoon	6 g
sweetened condensed milk	⅓ cup	75 ml
egg, at room temperature, lightly beaten	1	

1. In the bowl of a food processor fitted with the blade attachment, pulse together the flour, butter, and salt until the mixture resembles cornmeal.

2. In a small bowl, whisk together the condensed milk and egg. While pulsing, slowly pour this into the flour until the dough just comes together.

3. Turn the dough out onto a lightly floured work surface and gently turn over a few times until it is smooth, the dry ingredients have been completely integrated, and the dough holds together. Take care not to overwork it.

4. Shape the dough into a loose circle, cover it with plastic wrap, and allow to rest in the refrigerator for at least 20 minutes.

Hand Pie Dough

THIS IS A ZIPPY AND EASY-TO-HANDLE DOUGH, TAILOR-MADE FOR SMALL, HANDHELD TREATS. It translates well to both sweet and savory, baked and fried.

all-purpose flour, cold	2 cups	250 g
baking powder	1 teaspoon	5 g
salt	½ teaspoon	3 g
vegetable shortening, frozen	3 tablespoons	40 g
unsalted butter, cut into small pieces and chilled	2 tablespoons	30 g
milk	½ cup	120 ml
sweetened condensed milk	¼ cup	60 ml

1. In a food processor, pulse together the flour, baking powder, and salt.

2. Add the shortening and butter. Pulse until the mixture resembles cornmeal.

3. Whisk together the milk and condensed milk.

4. With the processor running, slowly add the milk mixture and continue to pulse until the dough just comes together.

5. Turn the dough out onto a large piece of plastic wrap. Use the plastic wrap to turn the dough over a few times, until it no longer has dry bits of flour visible and is smooth. It's important that the dough be rather smooth; otherwise, when you roll it out for your crust, the dough will crack.

6. Wrap the dough in the plastic wrap and let it rest in the refrigerator for at least 20 minutes before using.

OPTION!

Oatmeal makes for a rustic and nutty addition to hand pie dough. Replace ¼ cup (30 g) of the all-purpose flour with ¼ cup (20 g) of ground instant oatmeal.

Quick Puff Pastry

PUFF PASTRY IS CALLED PUFF BECAUSE IT PUFFS! It's true. The procedure of folding the butter in "turns," as shown on page 27, a process known as lamination, creates alternating layers of butter encased in flour. When touched by the heat of your oven, these become puffed layers of infinite flakiness. The resulting pastry is glorious and unruly—and perfect with custards, which, at their heart, are astoundingly rich and sweet. The Quick Puff crust, with its insane buttery crispness, puts what could otherwise be over-the-top sugary creaminess in its place.

This version is called "quick" (or "blitz") because you cut the butter into the dough instead of going through a proper lamination, as you do with Traditional Puff Pastry (page 25). You also make all the folds and turns at once instead of resting in between, as in the traditional method.

You can substitute Quick Puff for All-Butter or Part-Butter Easy Pie Dough (page 19) as well, if you're feeling reckless abandon. Either way, flavor- and texture-wise, there's nothing quite like it.

Makes approximately 4 pounds 11 ounces (2.1 kg) dough

all-purpose flour, cold	2 pounds (7½ cups)	910 g
salt	½ teaspoon	3 g
unsalted butter, chilled and cut into small pieces	2 pounds	910 g
cold water	1¼ cups	300 ml

1. In a large bowl, combine the flour, salt, and butter.

2. Massage the butter into the flour with the tips of your fingers until the butter pieces are a bit smaller, about the size of a dime. Add the water and smoosh everything around with a wooden spoon or with your hands, coating the mixture with water (this gets terribly messy

and sticky). Gently knead until the whole mess looks like it's just barely holding together. Dump the dough out onto a lightly floured surface and form it into a loose square. (See image A.)

3. Cover the dough with plastic wrap and let it rest for 10 minutes on the counter, where the flour will continue to absorb moisture from the water and the butter. Then roll it out gently, sprinkling flour on your work surface and your rolling pin to keep everything from sticking.

4. Roll the dough into a rough 12-by-20-inch (30.5-by-50-cm) rectangle (see image B). Make a single fold by bringing one short edge of the dough to the midline of the rectangle (see image C), then fold the other side over on top of the first fold (see image D)—just like folding a letter (that's why this process is also called a letter fold)! Turn the dough 90 degrees (see image E), roll the dough out again to the same size rectangle, and make another letter fold. Do this twice more, to make 4 folds and turns in total (see images F and G). This is a holy mess until you get to the last turn. Bits are going to plop off willy-nilly. Don't worry. Just be patient. Shove the errant dough chunks back into the whole and persevere! (See image H.)

5. Cover the dough with plastic wrap and allow to rest in the refrigerator for at least 20 minutes before using.

A NOTE FROM THE SWEETIE PIE

Delicate crusts like quick puff often slough down around the edges during blind baking. Here's a trick to prevent this from happening: Lay a sheet of parchment on top of your chilled dough in the pie plate; then, instead of weighing down with pie weights, stack another like-size pie plate on top. Flip the two sandwiched pie plates over onto a sheet pan and bake the crust, upside down, for 20 minutes.

Baking a double crust is tricky. Why? Well, you're filling an unbaked round of dough with a wet filling and praying to the baking saints that the bottom crust will actually feel some of the heat from the oven and, fingers crossed, will bake through and not come out in a gummy mess.

This is how you give yourself a leg up when it comes to baking the double crust:

First, use a glass pie dish (I use Pyrex) to bake the pie. This allows you to *see* the bottom of the pie and discern whether there is any coloring to the dough, which would indicate that it's actually baked through.

Second, dock the bottom crust (i.e., poke holes in the bottom crust with a fork to allow the bottom to vent and the hot air to circulate) and then sprinkle your bottom crust with Crust Dust before you add the filling. Crust Dust is a fifty-fifty mixture of sugar and flour. I keep a container of it on my counter and sprinkle a tablespoon or two (10 to 20 g) on my bottom crust, just enough to create an even dusting, before I add the filling. This creates a bit of absorbing action at the bottom of the crust to give your raw dough a little barrier from the wet stuff that's weighing it down. Another option is to brush the bottom crust with a little egg white and bake until the egg white has lost its glossy sheen before adding the filling. This also creates a barrier.

Third, roll out the top crust or gently stretch the lattice so that it's large enough to cover the entire filling and extends to cover the edges of the bottom crust so that the top and bottom crusts can be neatly crimped together.

Third, freeze your unbaked pie before baking it. That way, the crusts, since they are on the outside, will start to cook first. The baking process will take longer, but it's a small price to pay for the guarantee of a crispy double crust.

Fourth, bake until the top crust is a dark golden brown and the filling actually bubbles up and around the upper crust. This gives you an indication that the whole pie, including the innards, has gotten hot enough for the bottom crust to have felt the lick of some heat.

Fifth, when you're fairly certain that the filling has gotten there and you *think* the bottom crust has gotten some baking time in, leave it for a few minutes extra and—just as you want to take out the pie—place it on the bottom of the oven for five minutes. No, not the bottom rack—on the actual *bottom* of the oven. This is your extra guarantee that you won't end up with a gorgeous pie with a raw dough bottom.

Traditional Puff Pastry

***MILLE-FEUILLE*.** **PUFF PASTRY. "A THOUSAND LAYERS" IN FRENCH; A CLOUD OF DELICIOUS DELICACY TO ENGLISH SPEAKERS.** For everyone, a decadent butter delivery system—one that is flaky, tasty, and unadulterated glory in pastry form. I'm sure you'll be tempted to replace all the other piecrust options with this one beautiful dough, but let me just put this out there now: It's pointless to use puff pastry as a traditional piecrust.

Puff needs her space. She needs room to breathe, room to move, and if you ladle heavy fillings on top of the raw dough, you'll crush all her potential. That's why she's such a great choice for things like Apple Tarte Tatin (page 86), where the dough is set *atop* the filling so she can do her puffing thing, or napoleon-inspired pastries (pages 237 and 242), where she's left to rise all on her own before you fill 'er up with all manner of creamy goodness.

The best thing about puff is that when you want to elevate pie, when you have need for a showpiece that shines on the table as well as in your mouth, puff pastry offers a way to build desserts worthy of serving as a centerpiece.

Makes 5 pounds (2.3 kg) of pastry

FOR THE BUTTER BLOCK		
unsalted butter, at room temperature	2 pounds	910 g
salt	1 teaspoon	6 g
lemon juice	1 teaspoon	5 ml
bread flour, cold	8 ounces (½ pound)	225 g
FOR THE DOUGH		
salt	2 teaspoons	12 g
lemon juice	2 teaspoons	10 ml
unsalted butter, melted and cooled	½ cup	115 g
all-purpose flour, cold	1½ pounds	680 g

The butter block and the dough should be the same temperature and consistency. Both should be cool and easy to handle. The butter should be firm enough that you can pick it up and transfer it from hand to hand, but not so cold and firm that it cracks when you bend it. It should be malleable, but not squishy. It's persnickety, I know, but taking the time to get your elements in sync is key to making perfect puff pastry.

Procedure for the butter block

1. In the bowl of a stand mixer fitted with the paddle attachment, combine the butter, salt, lemon juice, and bread flour. Mix until smooth.

2. Using a plastic bowl scraper, transfer the butter to a piece of 12-by-16-inch (30.5-by-40.5-cm) parchment. Form the butter into a 10-by-14-inch (25-by-35.5-cm) rectangle in the middle of the parchment, using a small offset spatula to even it out on the top and sides. Place a second piece of parchment over the top of the butter and fold the extra parchment over the sides to seal the butter block and form a neat package. Tape down the sides of the parchment bundle with masking tape and then wrap the entire package tightly in plastic wrap. Use a rolling pin to continue to even out the butter, pressing gently so that it fills out the square edges of the packet; don't press so hard that the butter squirts out of the sides, though. (See image A on page 27.) Refrigerate for no longer than 20 minutes.

Procedure for the dough

1. In the bowl of an electric mixer fitted with the dough hook, combine the salt, 1¾ cups (420 ml) water, and the lemon juice. Stir. Add the melted butter and flour and mix on low until the dough is smooth. This is a rather soft and wet dough.

At my pastry shop in Montpelier, I once witnessed a sight that almost brought me to my knees with anguish. My helper, an experienced chef and one-time culinary school instructor, was rolling out quick puff for pies against the layers. *Sacré bleu!* After all the work of folding the dough and creating layers of butter, he proceeded to mash the dough in exactly the wrong way.

"Lamination" is the perfect description of the process of making traditional puff pastry because it's just like laminating a piece of paper. Think of the dough as the plastic and the butter block as the paper itself. You seal the butter into the protective casing of the dough. In the case of puff pastry, you don't stop there, but you continue folding and turning so that you create *many* layers of dough and butter and dough and butter and dough and butter. When you cut a piece of dough to roll it out, take a look at a cross section and you'll actually *see* the layers!

When rolling out puff pastry—the quick as well as the traditional—you must make sure to roll with the layers, not against them. Roll so that you are pressing down on the layers horizontally, keeping them stacked one upon the other. That way, they

will expand and puff when the heat of the oven hits the pastry dough. Roll the dough any other way, and you are squashing the layers into disarray, transforming your puff to *pfffft*.

First, make sure that your work surface has an even layer of flour so that your dough doesn't stick and tear during the process. Make the dough as even as humanly possible when you roll it; only this will ensure beautiful and uniform layers. **Second,** be sure to allow the dough to rest between turns. Rolling out the dough works the glutens and makes the dough tough to handle immediately after a turn. Allowing it to rest makes it easier to handle during the next turn.

2. Transfer the dough to a parchment-lined sheet pan that's been sprayed with nonstick spray. Gently spread the dough with your hands to form a rough rectangle and cover it with plastic wrap. Allow it to rest for 30 minutes in the refrigerator.

Lamination

1. Turn the dough out onto an evenly floured work surface. Roll it into a 16-by-24-inch (40.5-by-61-cm) rectangle. As you roll, check to be sure that it isn't sticking to your work surface.

2. Unwrap your butter block. Place it on one half of the dough rectangle, leaving a border of dough free along the edges of the butter (see image B). Fold the other half of the dough over and press down on the dough edges to seal in the butter (see images C and D). This process is called the "lock-in" because you are literally locking the butter into a dough package.

3. Turn the dough so the long side is facing you and again roll it into a 16-by-24-inch (40.5-by-61-cm) rectangle (see image E), making sure that it is very even and the edges are straight. I often use a sharp knife to trim the edges to make the rectangle perfect. (See image F.)

4. Fold one short edge of the dough to the midline of the rectangle (see image G) and then fold the remaining third over on top to make a single or letter turn (see image H). Just like folding a letter!

5. Cover the dough with plastic wrap and refrigerate it for at least 20 but no longer than 30 minutes (if you keep the dough too long in the fridge, the butter will harden and crack as you roll it out, so be on top of your timing).

6. Turn the dough back out onto your lightly floured work surface and repeat steps 3 through 5 three more times, so that you have made 4 letter turns in total, taking care to allow the dough to rest in between turns for 20 to 30 minutes in the refrigerator.

7. Once you've finished your last turn, cover the dough with plastic wrap and allow it to rest in the refrigerator for at least 1 hour before using it. (See image I.)

Option!

For a chocolate puff pastry, when mixing the dough, add ⅔ cup (60 g) cocoa powder to the flour.

A NOTE FROM THE SWEETIE PIE

You'll notice that the recipes for both quick puff and traditional puff make a fair bit more than you need for a single pie. I've done this for a few reasons.

First, the techniques used in both processes require a decent amount of dough to work correctly.

Second, the dough freezes beautifully; you need only thaw it in the refrigerator for an hour or so before getting to work.

Third, the procedure, especially for traditional puff, is slightly labor-intensive and time-consuming (but totally worth it). If you're taking the time, make enough to have on hand in the freezer for emergency hors d'oeuvres or a last-minute dessert.

There's no secret to working with pie and tart doughs, but there are tricks: Be gentle, keep everything cool, use just enough flour to keep the dough from sticking to your work surface, and allow doughs to rest before rolling and before baking them. You don't need fancy accessories to make things beautiful. You just need a rolling pin, patience, and a few tricks of the trade:

Use just enough flour on your cool work surface to ensure that your dough doesn't stick. Gently dust your rolling pin with flour as well, because the dough can stick on the bottom *and* the top.

Roll the dough from the middle out, using even strokes. Rotate the dough in increments of about an eighth of a turn after each stroke with the rolling pin; this way, you'll end up with a close-to-perfect round for your crust. Trim the round to keep the circle of dough neat.

Transport the finished round carefully. Roll it loosely onto your rolling pin to transfer it to the pie plate. This keeps the dough intact and keeps it from stretching.

Leave an inch overhang when lining the bottom of a pie plate. For a single-crust pie, tuck the overlap under and then crimp the edges. For a double crust, gently crimp the top and bottom edges together and then tuck under any dough that's hanging over. I make it a point *never* to allow the edge of my crust to extend much beyond the edge of the actual pie pan. For terribly tender doughs, the edges tend to fall off. Let the pie plate work for you, with the rim of the baking dish acting as a prop to keep the delicate crimped edges in place.

Sweet Tart Dough

I'LL ADMIT IT; I EAT THIS DOUGH RAW. It's the best kind of cookie dough that's really the best kind of piecrust. I use it for everything from all-American Lemon Tartlets (page 166) to the European classic Apricot Tart (page 73). Anything that can use a little buttery sweetness does well with this yummy crust.

Makes just under 2 pounds (910 g) dough, enough for 2 (9-inch/22-cm) crusts or 4 (4-inch/10-cm) crusts

all-purpose flour, cold	2 cups	250 g
cornstarch	1 cup	130 g
sugar	½ cup	100 g
salt	1 teaspoon	6 g
unsalted butter, cold	1¼ cups	285 g
egg	1	
sweetened condensed milk	3 tablespoons	45 ml
vanilla bean paste or vanilla extract	1 teaspoon	5 ml

1. In the bowl of a food processor fitted with the blade attachment, pulse together the flour, cornstarch, sugar, and salt. Add the butter and pulse until the mixture resembles coarse cornmeal.

2. In a small bowl, whisk together the egg, condensed milk, and vanilla. Slowly add the egg mixture to the flour mixture while pulsing; continue until the dough just begins to come together.

3. Turn the dough out onto a lightly floured surface. Gently knead it until the dry ingredients are fully integrated and the dough holds together, being careful not to overwork it.

4. Form the dough into a disk, wrap it in plastic, and refrigerate it for at least 30 minutes.

A NOTE FROM THE SWEETIE PIE

Some doughs aren't meant to be rolled out and easily transferred to your pie or tart tin. You know the ones I'm talking about, the ones that crumble and tear the second you think about lifting them from your work surface. Sweet doughs are notorious for being hard to handle, but there's a trick: Accept immediately that you are going to be pressing it into place with your fingers. Embrace this as a time-saver. If you can get past your own urge to roll it out, simply bypass that step and go straight to breaking off pieces of dough and pressing them into your tart ring.

OPTIONS!

Option 1 Citrus
For lemon (Meyer and traditional) and lime (Key and Persian), the zest of 1 lime or lemon mixed into the dough is perfect. For orange or grapefruit, 1 tablespoon (6 g) will do.

Option 2 Hazelnut or Macadamia Nut
Replace ¼ cup (32 g) of the cornstarch with ¼ cup (28 g) chopped roasted hazelnuts or chopped macadamia nuts. Pulse along with the flour and the cornstarch as instructed in step 1, to reduce the nuts to a fine meal.

Option 3 Chocolate
Replace 2 tablespoons (16 g) of the cornstarch with dark cocoa powder.

Option 4 Semolina
Trade out 1 cup (125 g) of the all-purpose flour for 1 cup of semolina flour.

Option 5 Green Tea (Matcha) or Espresso
Add 1 tablespoon (3 g) green tea powder or freshly and very finely ground espresso beans along with the flour.

Option 6 Anise
Whisk ½ teaspoon anise extract into the egg mixture.

Chocolate Cookie Tart Crust

THIS IS A SCRUMPTIOUS AND ELEGANT CHOCO-
LATE TART DOUGH. The key is using the right cocoa
powder. You can't go with your grocery-store variety of
anemic cocoa. No, sir. I'll know if you use it, too. You
must use a high-quality, very dark cocoa: Cacao Barry
or Valrhona are excellent choices. For this one, I use
Cacao Barry Extra Brute. You'll thank me later.

*Makes enough dough for 2 (8-inch/20-cm) tarts,
8 (4-inch/10-cm) tarts, or 16 mini tarts*

eggs	2	
sweetened condensed milk	2 tablespoons	30 ml
brewed coffee, cooled	2 tablespoons	30 ml
all-purpose flour, cold	1½ cups	185 g
cocoa powder	½ cup	40 g
sugar	¾ cup	150 g
instant espresso powder (optional; see Note, page 142)	1 tablespoon	3 g
salt	1 teaspoon	6 g
unsalted butter, cut into small pieces and chilled	¾ cup	180 g

1. In a small bowl, whisk together the eggs, condensed milk, and coffee.

2. In the bowl of a food processor fitted with the blade attachment, pulse together the flour, cocoa, sugar, espresso powder (if using), and salt.

3. Add the butter and pulse until the mixture resembles course cornmeal. While pulsing, add the liquid ingredients, and continue until the dough just holds together when you press it with your fingers.

4. Turn the dough out onto a large piece of plastic wrap. Form it into a flat disk, cover it completely with the plastic wrap, and refrigerate it for at least 30 minutes.

Strudel Dough

STRUDEL DOUGH IS AS THIN AS RICE PAPER,
PERHAPS THINNER. The guide when making (actually, stretching) strudel dough is that it's perfect when
you can read a newspaper through it. It should be used
at once as it dries out very quickly, and the key to using
it successfully is to layer it so that it forms a flaky whirlwind of deliciousness.

Makes 1¾ pounds (800 g) strudel dough

bread flour or other high-gluten flour, cold	1 pound, plus 1 or 2 ounces more, if needed	455 g, plus 30 or 60 g more, if needed
unsalted butter, very soft	3 tablespoons	42 g
vegetable oil	3 tablespoons, plus extra to prevent sticking	45 ml, plus extra to prevent sticking
salt	1½ teaspoons	9 g
water, room temperature	1½ cups, plus 1 or 2 ounces more, if needed	360 ml, plus 30 or 60 ml more, if needed
FOR THE FINISH		
unsalted butter, melted	1 cup	225 g

1. In the bowl of a stand mixer fitted with a dough hook, combine the flour, butter, oil, salt, and 1½ cups (360 ml) water. Mix until the dough comes together into a smooth and elastic mass. The dough should pull away from the sides of the bowl but still be very sticky and terribly soft. When you handle it, though, it should not stick to your hands. Work the dough for at least 15 to 20 minutes in the mixer. If it is still too sticky after that, add a little more flour. If the dough is too dry, add a little more water. Add only a very small amount of either at a time.

2. Coat the dough with the vegetable oil and cover the bowl with plastic wrap. Allow it to rest in a warm area for 2 hours.

3. Stretch the dough. For any strudel dough recipe, the stretch is exactly the same: Clear your kitchen or dining-room table and cover it with a very large, clean, cotton tablecloth. Sprinkle the tablecloth with an even layer of flour. Take off any jewelry you wear on your hands—rings, watches, or bracelets, anything at all that might tug at the dough while you are working on it. Even better, make sure your fingernails are very short and well trimmed.

4. Place the dough on the tablecloth, in the very center of the table. Gently rub a heavy rolling pin with oil and roll the dough into a rectangle approximately 2 feet by 1 foot (61 by 30.5 cm). Make sure that the dough isn't sticking to the cloth.

5. Start stretching by gently tugging on the ends of the dough. (See images A and B.) Try as hard as you can not to tear the dough. If you end up with a few nicks and tears, it's not the end of the world, but it's best if you pull with the intent of creating one glorious piece of ludicrously thin dough without blemish. Once you have doubled the original size of the rectangle, gently put your hands under the dough, palms up, and stretch it using a hand-over-hand motion. (See image C.) Continue in this way, aiming to create an even thinness over the entire dough sheet. The very edges can remain a little thick; that way you have something to hold on to when you pull (and you'll end up trimming the edges anyway).

For the finish

1. Once the dough, in its entirety, is thin enough to read through, you've reached the perfect stretch. My dining-room table is the ideal size—68 by 32 inches (1.72 m by 81 cm)—the dough fits on it entirely and sometimes drapes over a bit.

2. Work quickly at this point to complete the pastry of your choice, because the dough *will* dry out. Once the dough is stretched, I take a scissor or a very sharp knife and cut the thicker edges off the preimiter and discard them. And then I *very gently* brush the dough with melted butter.

Pizza Dough

THIS IS A DOUGH THAT'S PERFECT FOR ALL
PIZZA TOPPINGS. It can be stretched to the point that
it's cracker-thin and crispy when baked, or stretched a
little less so that it's slightly chewy yet crackly where
it counts. Play with your dough; let your kids get their
hands on it. Don't be precious and don't fret if it isn't
perfectly round—it will still be perfectly delicious.

Makes enough for 1 (10-inch/25-cm) pie

dry yeast	1 (¼-ounce) package	1 (7-g) package
lukewarm water	¾ cup	180 ml
all-purpose flour, cold	1½ cups	185 g
salt	1 teaspoon	6 g
sugar	½ teaspoon	2 g
vegetable oil	1 tablespoon	15 ml
cornmeal, for the pizza peel		

1. In the bowl of a stand mixer fitted with the dough hook,
   stir the yeast together with the water. Leave the yeast
   to bloom (that is, dissolve and foam), about 5 minutes.

2. Add the flour, salt, and sugar. Mix on medium-low until
   an elastic, smooth, and shiny dough forms, at least 10
   minutes.

3. Transfer the dough to a large bowl that's been coated
   with the vegetable oil. Turn the dough over a few times
   so that every surface receives a light coating of oil. With
   a sharp serrated knife, cut a cross in the dough. Cover
   it with plastic wrap or a damp kitchen towel and allow
   it to rest in a warm corner until it has doubled in size,
   1 to 2 hours.

4. Lightly dust your work surface with flour and gently flatten the dough with the palm of your hand. Roll
   it out into a rough 10- to 11-inch (25- to 28-cm) round
   between ⅛ and ¼ inch (3 and 6 mm) thick. Don't worry

if it's not perfectly round . . . or even barely round. Just
make sure that it's of a uniform thickness, even if it's the
shape of a beaver tail.

5. Sprinkle a pizza peel with cornmeal and transfer the
   dough to the peel. If you don't have a peel, use the
   back of a sheet pan instead (use the back so the dough
   slips off easily and isn't impeded by the lip of the working side).

A NOTE FROM THE SWEETIE PIE
Why a Pizza Stone?

Well, you could use a baking sheet coated in oil or
covered with parchment. Either works as a surface
for baking the pizza dough and keeping it from
sticking. However, the point of a great pizza crust,
like any great pie dough, is that the stuff actually
bakes through. With pizza, it's best when the dough
gets a nice crisp to it. Pizza stones distribute heat
evenly and extract excess moisture, producing the
perfect crust. If you're going to take the time to
make the right dough, do some legwork and get
a pizza stone so that it bakes right too. (The cheap
ones work just as well as the expensive ones—or
you can use a large unglazed or untreated terra-
cotta tile.)

a few

MASTER RECIPES

Pastry Cream

PASTRY CREAM IS A STAPLE IN EVERY BAKER'S REFRIGERATOR. At Gesine Confectionary, I made ten-pound batches daily that I then flavored and lightened to create fillings for everything from cream puffs and éclairs to napoleons to cakes. The stuff is so damn delicious, it's tough to stop yourself from taking a spoon to it and finishing it off straight away . . . which is an option, of course. This recipe can be doubled or tripled without fear (you can also halve it, but I can't imagine you'd want *less*).

Makes approximately 2½ cups (600 ml)

heavy cream	1 cup	240 ml
whole milk	1 cup	240 ml
sugar	½ cup	100 g
cornstarch	¼ cup	32 g
egg yolks	6	
salt	½ teaspoon	3 g

1. In a heavy-bottomed saucepan, bring the cream and milk to a simmer over medium heat. At the same time, in the bowl of an electric mixer fitted with the whisk attachment, whisk together the sugar, cornstarch, egg yolks, and salt until smooth and well combined.

2. With the mixer still running on low, to prevent splashing, carefully pour the hot milk/cream mixture down the side of the mixing bowl and into the sugar/egg yolk mixture. Raise the speed to high and beat until the ingredients are well blended.

3. Transfer the mixture back into the saucepan, scraping the sides of the bowl to make sure you get all the stray bits of cornstarch and sugar. Whisk the custard over medium heat until it thickens to the consistency of mayonnaise.

4. Transfer the pastry cream to a large bowl and cover it with plastic wrap. Place the wrap directly on the surface of the pastry cream so skin won't form. Refrigerate the pastry cream until cool, about 2 hours. Pastry cream thick-ens *considerably* as it cools. This is normal! Before using it, stir it vigorously to make it spreadable and smooth again.

OPTIONS!

Option 1 Salted Caramel Pastry Cream
Place the sugar in a heavy saucepan with ¼ cup (60 ml) water and a drop of lemon juice and cook over medium-low heat, stirring constantly. When the sugar has completely melted, increase the heat to medium-high and cook until it's a medium amber. Immediately add the cream and milk and cook, stirring, until the mixture is completely combined. Whisk together the egg yolks, cornstarch, and 1 teaspoon (5 g) sea salt (increasing the salt content) and proceed with step 2.

Option 2 Fruit or Espresso Pastry Cream
Add ¼ cup (60 ml) fruit puree or 1 tablespoon (3 g) instant espresso powder when you combine the milk and cream.

Option 3 Green Tea Pastry Cream
Stir 1 tablespoon (3 g) matcha (green tea powder) into the pastry cream just before you refrigerate it.

Option 4 Coconut Pastry Cream
Replace the whole milk with coconut milk.

Option 5 Banana Pastry Cream
Just as the pastry cream begins to thicken, add ¼ cup (60 ml) banana syrup (I like Monin or Fabbri brands).

Option 6 Chocolate Pastry Cream
Stir ½ to 1 cup (120 ml to 240 ml) of softened chocolate ganache (page 37) into pastry cream prior to refrigeration.

Option 7 Pumpkin Pastry Cream
Stir in 1 cup (240 ml) pumpkin puree, 1 teaspoon (3 g) cinnamon, ¼ teaspoon (1 g) nutmeg, ¼ teaspoon (1 g) ground ginger, and ¼ teaspoon (1 g) ground cloves into warm pastry cream just before refrigerating.

Caramel

THERE ARE TWO TYPES OF CARAMEL WE'LL BE PLAYING WITH, A CLEAR CARAMEL THAT ACTS AS A HARD GLAZE (AS IN THE GÂTEAU ST. HONORÉ, PAGE 128) AND A SOFTER CARAMEL FOR FILLINGS (AS IN THE CHOCOLATE FLEUR DE SEL CARAMEL TART, PAGE 153).

Clear Caramel for Glazing

Makes approximately 1 cup (240 ml)

sugar	1 cup	200 g
lemon juice	1 squirt	

1. Stir together the sugar, ⅓ cup (75 ml) water, and the lemon juice in a heavy saucepan over medium-low heat until the sugar has completely melted. Brush the sides of the pan down with a dampened pastry brush to get rid of any errant sugar crystals. These crystals have a habit of jumping into the sugar syrup and sparking a crystallization process that essentially turns your sugar into a strange rock candy cavern and ruins your pot.

2. Stop stirring, increase the heat to high, and cook the sugar until it turns a medium-light amber. Take it off the heat—the caramel will continue to cook and darken.

Soft Caramel Filling

Makes approximately 2 cups (480 ml)

sugar	1 cup	200 g
corn syrup	¼ cup	60 ml
salt	1 teaspoon	6 g
unsalted butter	2 tablespoons	28 g
heavy cream	⅓ cup	75 ml
vanilla bean paste	1 teaspoon	5 ml

1. In a large, heavy saucepan, combine the sugar, ⅓ cup (75 ml) water, the corn syrup, and salt and cook, stirring, over medium-low heat until the sugar has melted.

2. Brush down the sides of the pan with a damp pastry brush to eradicate any errant sugar crystals.

3. Stop stirring, increase the heat to medium-high, and clip on a candy thermometer. Heat the sugar syrup to 245°F (120°C).

4. Once the syrup has reached temperature, take the pan off the heat and carefully add the butter and cream. The mixture will bubble vigorously at first. Stand back and let the hot sugar do its molten dance. When the syrup has calmed, stir until the butter has completely melted. Add the vanilla and stir again. Pour the caramel immediately into your pastry vessel (or other vessel) of choice and allow it to cool and set completely, 1 to 2 hours.

Ganache

GANACHE IS A CHOCOLATE CONCOCTION THAT CAN BE USED AS A GLAZE OR A FILLING, WHIPPED INTO A SPREADABLE FROSTING, OR ALLOWED TO SET IN A BOWL AND THEN SCOOPED TO FORM TRADITIONAL CHOCOLATE TRUFFLES. The stuff is glorious and decadent. Make sure to use the highest-quality chocolate you can get your hands on, always semi- or bittersweet, and take care to chop it into small, uniform pieces so that it melts evenly when you add the hot cream mixture. The corn syrup brings an extra sheen to the ganache, but you can feel free to leave it out.

Makes approximately 1¼ cups (300 ml)

heavy cream	½ cup	120 ml
unsalted butter	2 tablespoons	28 g
corn syrup (optional)	1 tablespoon	15 ml
salt	pinch	
semisweet or bittersweet chocolate (I use Callebaut's 60/40), finely chopped	8 ounces	225 g

1. In a small saucepan, bring the cream, butter, corn syrup (if using), and salt to a simmer, making sure the butter melts completely.

2. Place the chocolate in a heatproof mixing bowl and pour the hot cream mixture over it. Allow everything to sit undisturbed for 5 minutes and then whisk until the ganache is smooth.

3. Use the ganache immediately as a glaze or allow it to set, covered with plastic wrap in the fridge, for at least an hour.

Fruit Glaze

FRUIT TARTS IN PASTRY SHOPS HAVE THE ADDED GLITZ OF GETTING DOSED WITH PROFESSIONAL PASTRY GLAZE; THIS KEEPS THEM SHINY AND SUCCULENT, EVEN AFTER HOURS IN THE COOLER. But you don't need to shell out a ton of money or scour the internet for a specialized source for pastry glaze. You can go old-school and use the original glazing material: apricot preserves. The flavor is mild enough that it won't distract from the fruit it's coating.

Makes approximately ¼ cup (60 ml)

smooth apricot preserves	¼ cup	60 ml

1. Simply stir together the preserves and 2 tablespoons (30 ml) water in a small saucepan over low heat until the preserves have melted and the mixture is smooth.

2. Brush this on your fruits with a small pastry brush and sit back and enjoy the compliments.

CHAPTER

2

the

SWEETS

Sweet is where American pies live—in the lattice tops and double crusts and the fruits and creams that dwell beneath them. Start with a decision about the crust: Do you want it *über* flaky? I'd go with quick puff. Flaky and tender? The obvious choice is the all-butter pie dough. Just tender and keeps its shape? Try the part-butter/part-shortening pie dough. Sweet? That's the perfect time to use sweet tart dough. Buttery? I think that's the ideal opportunity to break out the simple tart crust!

Next it's time to master fillings. Let's make that filling stand straight up and shout "howdy" when you slice into it instead of letting loose a flood of goo that slides around the pie tin. Let's see those berries stay together when you heat them without making a jam. Let's bring life to a strawberry-rhubarb filling! I say we make a cream pie that doesn't taste like a Cool Whip catastrophe!!

Once we have these skills, we can play in ways you never thought possible. Whether you're making a full-scale sliceable pie for an entire family or a tiny individual tart, it's all about flavor.

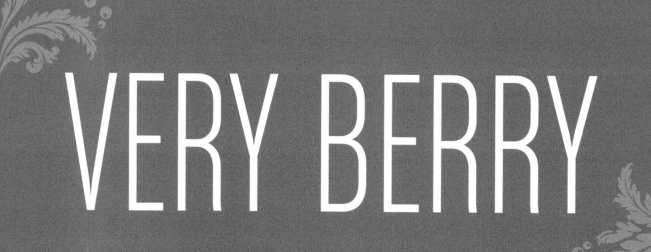

VERY BERRY

A GALETTE IS A FREE-FORM PIE, A LOVELY ROUND OF DOUGH, ITS CENTER PILED HIGH WITH FRUITY GOODNESS AND ITS EDGES SIMPLY TUCKED UP AND OVER TO FORM A MAKESHIFT DAM TO KEEP THAT GOODNESS FROM FLOWING OUT. In the height of summer, when the berries are falling from our bushes, we pick buckets of black raspberries. While we usually eat two for every one we drop into the bucket, those that actually make it into the house will be baked into a galette. You see, if I take the time to make a double-crust pie or a fancy tart, I'll end up polishing off the rest of the berries before you can say "lattice."

And since there are other New England comestibles hanging around, begging to be included—like the leftover whole cranberries in the freezer, a few stalks of rhubarb still straggling on the bush outside the kitchen door, and a pint of strawberries hanging out on the kitchen counter—I'll toss them into the mix and have a ruby-red galette ready just in time for afternoon coffee.

New England
BERRY
GALETTE

MAKES 1
(12-INCH/30.5-CM) GALETTE

Quick Puff Pastry (page 22)	⅛ batch	
chopped rhubarb	2 cups	245 g
cranberries	2 cups	230 g
granulated sugar	½ cup	100 g
zest of 1 lemon		
vanilla bean paste	1 teaspoon	5 ml
tapioca starch	2 tablespoons	15 g
black raspberries	1 pint	340 g
strawberries	1 pint	340 g
egg wash (1 egg whisked with 2 tablespoons/30 ml water)		
sanding sugar or turbinado sugar, for sprinkling	2 tablespoons	25 g

1. Preheat the oven to 350°F (175°C). Roll the pastry into a rough 14-inch (35.5-cm) round and place it on a baking sheet lined with parchment. Dock the middle of the dough and refrigerate it for at least 20 minutes.

2. Meanwhile, in a large pot over medium heat, combine the rhubarb, cranberries, sugar, zest, and vanilla. Cook until the fruit juices start flowing and start to simmer.

3. Ladle approximately ¼ cup (60 ml) of the juices from the pot into a small bowl and whisk in the tapioca starch. Pour the mixture back into

the pot and stir it into the fruit until combined. Bring the mixture to a simmer and gently stir in the black raspberries and strawberries. Set the pot aside to cool.

4. Remove the dough from the refrigerator and spoon the filling into the middle of the round, leaving a border of about 1 inch (2.5 cm) uncovered all around. Gently fold the edges of the dough over the fruit, leaving the majority of the fruit exposed, creating pleats as you go along.

5. Using a pastry brush, brush the egg wash over the exposed dough. Sprinkle the entire top with sanding or turbinado sugar. As an insurance policy, I'll place a cake ring the same size as the galette around the sides to provide extra stability and keep everything tidy.

6. Bake the galette for 35 to 40 minutes, until the crust is golden brown.

Raspberry
BAKEWELL
TART

MAKES 1
(10-INCH/25-CM) TART

A COOK SCREWS UP AT THE INN, AND A LEGENDARY TART IS BORN. This seems to be the way with pastry history: Someone too tired or too lazy to read directions properly ends up inventing a treat that surpasses the original. Usually it's the French who end up with the happy accidents, but this time the English get the honors with the Bakewell Tart, wherein, at the White Horse Inn in Derbyshire, England, the kitchen help were told to make a simple jam tart. They were just supposed to stir a few ingredients together and pour them into the tart shell. Instead, said help layered the ingredients in one by one without stirring, creating layers of color, flavor, and texture. It makes me wonder how many other things these culinary sloths messed up that turned out horribly . . . because we never hear about those.

FOR THE CRUST		
Sweet Tart Dough (page 30)	½ batch	
FOR THE FILLINGS		
raspberries	1 pint	340 g
granulated sugar, divided	1½ cup	300 g
unsalted butter	½ cup	115 g
eggs	3	
almond extract	½ teaspoon	2.5 ml
almond flour	1½ cups	210 g
salt	½ teaspoon	3 g
zest of 1 lemon		
FOR THE ASSEMBLY		
sliced, blanched almonds	¼ cup	23 g
egg white	1	
granulated sugar	1 tablespoon	25 g
confectioners' sugar, for dusting		

Procedure for the crust

1. Preheat the oven to 350°F (175°C). Line a 10-inch (25-cm) tart pan with the dough and freeze it for 20 minutes.

2. Line the crust with parchment, fill it with pie weights or dried beans, and bake it for 15 minutes. Remove the weights and parchment. Set the crust aside.

Procedure for the fillings

1. In a saucepan, combine the raspberries and ½ cup (50 g) of the sugar. Stir the mixture over medium heat until the sugar has completely melted, the juices begin to flow and bubble, and the sauce thickens, 10 to 15 minutes. Set it aside to cool.

2. In the bowl of an electric mixer fitted with the paddle attachment, cream together the remaining sugar and the butter until light and fluffy. Add the eggs, one at a time, and then the almond extract.

3. Gently fold in the almond flour, salt, and lemon zest. Mix until the ingredients are evenly distributed.

Assembly

1. Spread the raspberry sauce in an even layer on the bottom of the crust. Gently spoon the almond filling over the raspberry sauce and smooth it out with a small offset spatula. Bake the tart for 20 minutes.

2. Meanwhile, gently stir together the almonds, egg white, and sugar.

3. Remove the tart from the oven and sprinkle the almond mixture over the top. Bake for 15 more minutes, or until the almonds are golden.

4. Allow the tart to cool completely before dusting it with confectioners' sugar.

Raspberry-Lemon
COCONUT
Panna-Cotta
TARTLETS

MAKES 8
(4-INCH/10-CM) TARTLETS

PANNA COTTA IS ITALIAN FOR "COOKED CREAM." It's the simplest of puddings; it contains no eggs and is set with gelatin, which gives it a smooth texture that allows the full force of the cream to settle onto your tongue without distraction. The real beauty of panna cotta is that it pairs wonderfully with fruit. It's creamy without being heavy, and the slight undertones of coconut and lemon in this version bring a brightness that mingles perfectly with fresh raspberries. Settle all this goodness in a crispy tart shell, and your mouth will be very happy.

FOR THE PANNA COTTA		
unflavored gelatin	2 teaspoons	5 g
lemon juice	2 tablespoons	30 ml
half-and-half	1½ cups	360 ml
coconut milk, well stirred	½ cup	120 ml
granulated sugar	¼ cup	50 g
salt	pinch	
FOR THE FILLING		
mascarpone	1 cup	230 g
confectioners' sugar	¼ cup	25 g
lemon zest	1 teaspoon	2 g
FOR THE CRUSTS		
Simple Tart Dough (page 21)	½ batch	
FOR THE ASSEMBLY		
raspberries	2 pints	680 g
confectioners' sugar, for dusting	¼ cup	25 g
zest of 1 lemon, for dusting		

Procedure for the panna cotta

1. In a small bowl, sprinkle the gelatin evenly over the lemon juice. Allow it to sit for 5 minutes (the gelatin will soak up the liquid and look wet).

2. Cook the half-and-half, coconut milk, sugar, and salt in a heavy saucepan, stirring, over medium heat until the sugar has completely melted. Continue heating to a simmer. Take the mixture off the burner and immediately add the lemon/gelatin mixture. Stir until the gelatin has completely melted into the liquid.

3. Divide the panna-cotta mixture among 8 small tea or coffee cups that have been lightly coated with nonstick cooking spray. Chill them until the panna cotta is completely cool and set, at least 2 hours.

A NOTE FROM THE SWEETIE PIE

Fruits are juicy! The infinite beauty of biting into a ripe, fuzzy peach is the cascade of sweet nectar dribbling down your chin and onto your favorite T-shirt. That sweet mess is essential for a satisfying peach-eating experience. However, pies require a bit of juice wrangling—a little culinary aid in keeping delicate berries, plump apples, and juicy peaches from sliding out of the pie onto the floor once you slice into your gorgeous creation.

Different fruits require different levels of juice corralling. Some, like apples, have high doses of pectin, a natural thickener, and require only a very small amount of assistance in the jelling department. Blueberries, on the other hand, run wild when heated and need extra help staying put on your plate.

You'll notice a variety of thickening agents included in *Pie It Forward*, from flour to cornstarch to Clearjel. Each is specific to the recipe, so don't trade them out willy-nilly!

Procedure for the filling

In a small mixing bowl, whisk together the mascarpone, confectioners' sugar, and lemon juice until smooth. Refrigerate until needed for assembly.

Procedure for the crusts

1. Preheat the oven to 350°F (175°C). Divide the dough into 8 equal pieces and roll each into a round approximately 6 inches (15 cm) across. Line 8 (4-inch/10-cm) tart rings (I use flan rings) with the dough rounds. Trim excess dough that extends beyond the rim of the tart or flan ring with a sharp paring knife. Dock the dough and freeze the shells for 20 minutes.

2. Line the tart rings with parchment and fill them with pie weights or dried beans. Bake for 10 minutes. Remove the parchment and pie weights and bake for 10 more minutes, or until the bottoms of the tart crusts just begin to lightly brown. Set them aside to cool completely.

Assembly

1. Divide the filling among the tart shells and spread it evenly along the bottom with the back of a small spoon. Loosen the panna cottas by running a butter knife around the edge of each cup. Carefully turn each cup upside down over each tart shell so that the panna cotta unmolds on top of the filling.

2. Garnish the top with raspberries and dust lightly with confectioners' sugar. Sprinkle lemon zest over each. Serve immediately.

IN SEASON, STRAWBERRIES ARE SO SWEET AND TENDER THEY NEED NOTHING TO COAX THEM INTO DELICIOUSNESS. They stand alone on the yummy stage, and no amount of culinary fussing is going to make them shine any brighter. But I like to bring a few friends along for the ride, just to keep things interesting: a little buttery crust to add structure, a dab of creaminess to smooth the journey on your tongue, and a wisp of lemon and a dash of basil to perk the players up.

Strawberry TART

MAKES 1
(9-INCH/23-CM) SQUARE TART

FOR THE CRUST		
Simple Tart Dough (page 21)	½ batch	
FOR THE STRAWBERRY FILLING		
strawberries, hulled and sliced into eighths	1 pint	340 g
granulated sugar	¼ cup	50 g
zest of 1 lemon		
minced fresh basil	½ teaspoon	1 g
FOR THE CRÈME FRAÎCHE FILLING		
crème fraîche	1 cup	240 ml
confectioners' sugar	2 tablespoons	12 g
vanilla bean paste	½ teaspoon	2.5 ml
FOR THE ASSEMBLY		
strawberries	25	
Fruit Glaze (page 37)	1 batch	
heavy cream	1 cup	240 ml
confectioners' sugar	3 tablespoons	17 g

Procedure for the crust

1. Preheat the oven to 350°F (175°C). Roll the dough into a rough 11-inch (28-cm) square. Line a 9-inch (23-cm) square tart pan with the dough and trim any excess that extends beyond the rim of the tart pan with a sharp paring knife. Dock the bottom of the dough. Freeze it for 20 minutes.

2. Line the tart shell with parchment and fill it with pie weights or dried beans. Bake for 15 minutes. Remove the pie weights and parchment and bake for 10 minutes more, or until the bottom of the crust has started to brown and the dough is baked through. Set it aside to cool completely.

Procedure for the strawberry filling

In a medium mixing bowl, stir together the sliced strawberries, granulated sugar, lemon zest, and basil. Allow the berries to macerate for 15 to 20 minutes, long enough that the juices run freely and the sugar has melted completely.

Procedure for the crème fraîche filling

In another bowl, stir together the crème fraîche, confectioners' sugar, and vanilla until smooth and combined.

Assembly

1. Spoon the crème fraîche mixture into the pie shell and smooth it into an even layer along the bottom using an offset spatula. Ladle the macerated strawberries and their juice evenly on top of the crème fraîche, working to keep the layer relatively level because it will act as a base upon which the whole strawberry structure will stand.

2. Cut the green ends off the whole strawberries. With a pastry brush, paint each strawberry with the fruit glaze, then arrange in neat rows.

3. In the bowl of an electric mixer fitted with the whisk attachment (or by hand for a nice workout), whisk together the cream and confectioners' sugar just until you achieve stiff peaks. (Be careful not to overbeat the cream!) Transfer the whipped cream to a serving bowl so your guests can dollop at will.

4. Serve the pie immediately or refrigerate it until you're ready for it.

A NOTE FROM THE SWEETIE PIE

Whipped cream is a lovely addition to the top of any pie. It often even finds a way to nestle inside the filling. And if you've made your share of whipped cream, no doubt you've whipped it right over the edge from pie friendly to buttery toast topping at least once. Here's a trick to save your beautiful cream. If you've overwhipped it to the point that it is slightly curdled and buttery, add about ¼ cup (60 ml) heavy cream to the mess and whisk. The damage, assuming you've not gone too far, will reverse. You're welcome.

*Strawberry Rhubarb
Lattice Crumble Pie*

Berry Hand Pies

Strawberry Tart

Strawberry RHUBARB LATTICE Crumble Pie

MAKES 1
(9-INCH/23-CM) PIE

A PATCH OF RHUBARB GREW ON THE SIDE OF THE DIRT ROAD JUST A SHORT HOP FROM OUR HOUSE IN VERMONT. We'd walk our dogs a mile down the road, past bubbling brooks and prancing ponies, and—despite all the bucolic scenery—all I could think about was getting my grimy paws on a few ruby stalks without the neighbors catching me, so I could run home to pick a pint of wild strawberries in our backyard and start making a pie! The tart herbaceousness of the rhubarb combines perfectly with the bright sweetness of strawberries. Nestled in brown sugar, vanilla, and butter, and topped with lattice and sweet, crunchy crumbles, it screams summertime with every mouthful.

FOR THE FILLING		
rhubarb	10 stalks	
unsalted butter	4 tablespoons	55 g
brown sugar, firmly packed	1 cup	220 g
heavy cream	¼ cup	60 ml
bourbon	2 tablespoons	30 ml
vanilla bean paste	1 tablespoon	15 ml
zest of 1 lemon		
salt	pinch	
cornstarch	¼ cup	32 g
strawberries, hulled and sliced in half	4 pints	1.4 kg
FOR THE CRUST		
All-Butter Easy Pie Dough (page 19)	1 batch	
Crust Dust (see Note, page 24)	1 tablespoon	10 g
FOR THE CRUMBLE		
unsalted butter, melted	1 cup	225 g
granulated sugar	½ cup	100 g
brown sugar, firmly packed	½ cup	110 g
salt	½ teaspoon	3 g
all-purpose flour	2½ cups	310 g
egg wash (1 egg wisked with 2 tablespoons/30 ml water)		

Procedure for the filling

1. Chop the rhubarb into ½-inch (12-mm) slices. In a large sauté pan, sauté in the butter until softened. Add the brown sugar, cream, bourbon, vanilla, lemon zest, and salt, and stir until coated. Sprinkle with the cornstarch and stir until it dissolves. Take the pan off the heat and gently fold in the strawberries. Set it aside to cool.

Procedure for the crust

Preheat the oven to 350°F (175°C). Cut the dough in half and return one half to the refrigerator. Roll the other piece into a loose 11-inch (28-cm) round and use this to line a 9-inch (23-cm) pie plate. Allow the edges to hang over just a bit and dock the bottom of the dough. Sprinkle the Crust Dust on the bottom. Refrigerate the crust for 20 minutes.

Procedure for the crumble

In a large bowl, stir together the melted butter, granulated and brown sugars, salt, and flour. Keep working the crumbs with your spoon or your fingers until the butter is absorbed and the mixture forms clumps.

Assembly

1. Preheat the oven to 350°F (175°C). Roll out the remaining half of the dough into a rough rectangle, ⅛ to ¼ inch (3 to 6 mm) thick. Cut 6 strips about 1½ inches thick by 11 inches long (4 by 28 cm) and 5 strips about ½ inch thick by 11 inches long (12 mm by 28 cm). With the extra dough, cut out berry and leaf shapes, if you want to.

2. Pour the strawberry-rhubarb mixture into the pie shell. Sprinkle the crumble over the filling in an even layer.

3. Weave the dough strips over the filling and crumble, forming a lattice (see the picture on page 51). If you made decorative dough shapes, arrange them on top.

4. Brush the lattice with the egg wash.

5. Bake the pie for 45 to 50 minutes, or until the filling begins to bubble and the bottom crust has browned.

A NOTE FROM THE SWEETIE PIE

Top crusts are the tops, aren't they? They can make or break the look of a pie. I find that when the pie filling is extravagantly *high,* like in the large Vermont Apple Pie (page 91), you need only place a simple top crust with a vent hole over the filling. The spectacle of the height is all you need to make it gorgeous. In other cases, when volume isn't present, a little drama is welcome.

If you get your hands on some tools, making jaw-droppingly beautiful crusts is a snap. For my Gesine Confectionary Cherry Pie (page 75), I cut polka dots into the top crust using a large open pastry tip. For traditional lattice, I like to use different thicknesses of strips for added visual impact, as I have done in the Strawberry Rhubarb Lattice Crumble Pie (opposite). For a uniform lattice, like that atop pie pops (page 94), I use a lattice roller available from pastry supply shops like Pastry-chef.com. And I'm sure you've noticed that exquisite design on the Wild Blueberry Pie (page 56)—that's a pie stencil, also available at pastry supply shops (I got mine at the King Arthur Flour Baker's Shop). And then there's the Not-So-Traditional Apple Pie (page 83), for which I make the top crust from overlapping heart cutouts. Beautiful *and* delicious.

Berry HAND PIES

MAKES 8
(4-INCH/10-CM) HAND PIES

THIS IS WHERE "EASY AS PIE" REALLY MEANS SOMETHING. A hand pie is a pie made to fit into your hand (or pocket) so you can transport its goodness on your travels without getting the filling all over your person. A turnover is just another name for a hand pie; a calzone is a large version of a hand pie; a Cornish pasty is a savory hand pie. Bottom line is you can transform most of your favorite pies into portable pouches of goodness and hide them away in your purse or pocket to wait patiently (and cleanly) until hunger strikes.

Hand Pie Dough (page 21)	1 batch	
fresh strawberries	½ pint	170 g
granulated sugar	¼ cup	50 g
zest and juice of 1 lemon		
fresh rosemary, finely chopped	1 teaspoon	2 g
cornstarch	2 tablespoons	16 g
sea salt	pinch	
fresh raspberries, halved	1 cup	170 g
egg wash (1 egg whisked with 2 tablespoons/30 ml water)		
sanding sugar or turbinado sugar, for sprinkling		
confectioners' sugar	½ cup	50 g
milk	2 tablespoons	30 ml

1. Hull the strawberries. Cut them into small pieces, a bit larger than corn kernels. Combine the strawberries, sugar, lemon zest, and rosemary in a mixing bowl and stir until the strawberries are evenly coated with sugar. Allow to macerate until the sugar melts and the juices of the strawberries run freely.

2. Drain the strawberry juice into a small bowl. Add the lemon juice, then stir in the cornstarch until the mixture becomes a smooth slurry without lumps.

3. In a heavy-bottomed saucepan, combine the strawberries, the cornstarch slurry, and the salt. Stir over medium heat until the mixture bubbles and thickens, 5 to 10 minutes. Allow the filling to cool completely in the refrigerator, about 20 minutes.

4. Stir the raspberries into the strawberry mixture.

5. Preheat oven to 350°F (175°C). Divide the dough evenly into 12 pieces. Roll each piece into a 4-inch (10-cm) round and place the rounds on a parchment-lined sheet pan.

6. With a pastry brush, brush egg wash along the outside edge of the dough rounds. Place 1½ tablespoons (22.5 ml) of filling onto the middle of each round. Fold the dough over, creating a half moon, and seal the pastries by pressing gently along the edges of each with the tines of a fork. Brush the outsides of the pastries with egg wash and sprinkle with sanding or turbinado sugar.

7. Bake for 20 minutes or until golden brown. Allow the hand pies to cool completely.

8. Whisk together the confectioners' sugar and milk. With a clean pastry brush, brush each hand pie evenly with the glaze.

OPTIONS!

Option 1 Fruity Kitchen Sink

Most pie fillings—from apple to blueberry—work well in hand pies. Just make sure that the fruit pieces aren't too large for the small rounds of dough. Cut the fruit into pieces just larger than kernels of corn.

Option 2 Custard

Pastry cream that's been sitting in the fridge for a few days can be added and baked for a glorious custard hot pocket.

Option 3 Meat treats

Seasoned ground pork or beef or any minced meat filling is perfect for these little pockets of dough. Instead of sprinkling with sanding sugar, try large-grain sea salt.

Option 4 Fry it up

If you've sealed your hand pies really well, I suggest you fill a stockpot with 3 inches (7.5 cm) of vegetable oil and heat it to 350°F (175°C). Fry the hand pies on each side until they are a deep golden brown, about 2 minutes per side. Insanely delicious.

A NOTE FROM THE SWEETIE PIE

You can make a pie without a pie plate—you've noticed this already, I assume, considering that you've just perused a hand-pie recipe. But apart from the world of hand pies, there are tart pans, flan rings, and even cake rings that can stand in for run-of-the-mill pie plates. Rings, whether flan or cake, do not have bottoms, they are simply—well, rings. The benefit of going bottomless with your pan is that the bottom crust browns evenly along with the sides and top, since the heat doesn't have to penetrate both a sheet pan and a cake bottom to get to the crust. Cake rings come in many diameters and depths, so keep your mind open to various sizes and shapes for all pies. Just because my recipe says 9 or 10 inches (23 or 25 cm) doesn't mean you can't finagle the crust and filling to accommodate your own miniature-pie desires when you get your hands on a group of ten 2-inch (5-cm) tart pans. Just play accordingly with the amounts of dough and filling. You will find a bevy of tart pans and flan- and cake-ring choices at online restaurant-supply shops such as bakedeco.com, jbprince.com, and pastrychef.com.

I ONLY LIKE BLUEBERRY PIE WHEN THERE ARE DISCERN-
IBLE, WHOLE BLUEBERRIES HIDING UNDER THE CRUST,
JUST WAITING TO BURST IN MY MOUTH. If it's mushy or jammy,
I'm not happy. But give me a slice of sweet berry pie, warm enough to
slowly melt a scoop of Häagen-Dazs and full of completely intact little
blue orbs nestled in buttery crust, and I'm a blissful girl.

All-Butter or Part-Butter/Part-Shortening Easy Pie Dough (page 19; or ¼ batch Quick Puff Pastry, page 22)	1 batch	
blueberries	3 pints	1 kg
zest and juice of 1 lemon		
sugar	1 cup	200 g
Clearjel (see Note)	¼ cup	40 g
vanilla extract	1 teaspoon	5 ml
nutmeg	½ teaspoon	1.5 g
salt	pinch	
Crust Dust (see Note, page 24)	1 tablespoon	10 g
unsalted butter, cut into tiny pieces	2 tablespoons	28 g
egg wash (1 egg whisked with 2 tablespoons/30 ml water)		
sanding sugar or turbinado sugar for sprinkling		

1. Divide the dough into halves and return one piece to the refrigerator. Roll the remaining half into a circle approximately 11 inches (28 cm) in diameter, use it to line a 9-inch (23-cm) pie plate, and chill it while you make the filling.

2. Sort through, destem, wash, and dry the blueberries. Toss them in a bowl with the lemon juice and zest.

3. Stir together the sugar, Clearjel, vanilla, nutmeg, and salt. (You *must* stir the Clearjel with the sugar before adding it to the fruit.) Gently stir the sugar mixture into the blueberries to coat them evenly.

4. Remove the bottom crust from the fridge and sprinkle it with an even layer of Crust Dust. Add the blueberries and dot the top of the fruit with the small pieces of butter.

5. Preheat the oven to 350°F (175°C). Remove the second piece of dough from the fridge and roll it into a 10-inch (25-cm) round. Cut it decoratively (see Note on page 53) or make a simple vent. Place it on top of

WILD
Blueberry
PIE

MAKES 1
(9-INCH/23-CM) PIE

NOTE

Clearjel is a modified cornstarch that thickens moisture-
filled fruit fillings beautifully
without causing cloudiness; it
also allows the bright flavors to
really shine.

the blueberries. Tuck the edges in between the pie plate and the lower crust and crimp the edges together.

6. Brush the top crust with the egg wash and sprinkle it with sanding or turbinado sugar.

7. Bake for 55 minutes, or until the top crust is dark golden brown, the filling is bubbling, and the bottom crust has browned (you'll only see this if you're using a glass pie plate).

A NOTE FROM THE SWEETIE PIE

I have nothing against using frozen berries in pies. Freezing is a beautiful way to prolong a very short berry season and bring a little fruity sunshine into some dark winter days. However, I would like to impart some berry wisdom.

First, remember that in freezing a berry you are incorporating an extra dose of moisture that comes from the damp of your freezer and gets into the mix when you ultimately warm the berries during baking. Keep this added moisture in mind and adjust thickening ratios accordingly. Don't go overboard with adding cornstarch, flour, tapioca, or Clearjel, though. A scant tablespoon extra should do it.

Second, when making clafoutis, custards, or brown-butter-based pies that require the berry to be suspended in a wet batter, DO NOT use frozen berries. The added moisture will seep into the custard and tamper with its consistency. In the case of frozen berries like blueberries, the skin color will bleed as well, tinting the batter an unsightly azure.

Third, don't expect the filling to be as plump and the berries to maintain their shape the way they would if they were fresh. The process of freezing and thawing compromises the integrity of the berry, so it breaks down considerably more when heated. It'll still be delicious, just not as upstanding as the fresh version.

IF YOU MELT BUTTER LONG ENOUGH, IT SEPARATES INTO BUTTERFAT, MILK SOLIDS, AND WATER. If you've ever made clarified butter or ghee, you've skimmed off the pure butterfat and tossed the rest.

But ignore the separation as you leave that butter in your saucepan over a low heat, and you'll notice that the milk solids on the bottom of the pan begin to brown. This is a good thing and is what gives this tart its luscious, nutty flavor.

When baked, the inside of the filling is smooth and reminiscent of a nutty tapioca, while the outside is brown and crisp. Studded with blueberries, this tart is a simple and elegant way to showcase fruit in season.

Blueberry
BROWN-BUTTER TARTLETS

MAKES 6
(4-INCH/10-CM) INDIVIDUAL TARTS

FOR THE CRUSTS		
All-Butter Easy Pie Dough (page 19)	1 batch	
FOR THE FILLING		
eggs	2	
sugar	½ cup	100 g
vanilla bean paste	½ teaspoon	2.5 ml
salt	½ teaspoon	3 g
all-purpose flour	¼ cup	30 g
unsalted butter	½ cup	115 g
blueberries, picked over to get rid of the smooshy ones and destemmed	1 pint	340 g

Procedure for the crusts

1. Preheat the oven to 350°F (175C°). Cut the dough in two, making one piece twice as large as the second. Cover the smaller piece of dough with plastic wrap and refrigerate.

2. Cut the larger piece of dough into 6 even pieces. Roll each piece into a 6-inch (15-cm) circle and line six 4-inch-wide (10-cm-wide) by 2-inch-tall (5-cm-tall) fluted tart rings with the dough. Dock and refrigerate for 20 minutes.

3. Roll the remaining piece of dough into a rough rectangle approximately 24 inches (61 cm) long, a few inches wide, and 1/8 inch (3 mm) thick. Firmly roll a lattice cutter along the length of the dough. Gently spread the lattice (see page 94) to make sure the roller has sliced though the

dough properly, and using a small paring knife, slice any uncut areas that the lattice roller missed. Transfer to a parchment-lined sheet pan and refrigerate.

4. Remove the crusts from the refrigerator and line each with a round of parchment and fill with pie weights.

5. Bake the crusts for 15 minutes and set them aside, leaving the oven on.

Procedure for the filling

1. In a large mixing bowl, whisk together the eggs, sugar, vanilla, and salt. Sift the flour over the mixture and gently fold in.

2. In a saucepan over medium heat, melt the butter until it has browned. Watch carefully and stir often so it doesn't burn. Allow to cool slightly.

3. Whisking constantly, pour the browned butter into the egg mixture and continue whisking until it is fully incorporated.

4. Place the crusts on a sheet pan in a tight, neat row, making sure they are touching each other. Evenly divide the blueberries among the crusts and pour butter over the top of each tartlet.

Assembly

1. Gently transfer the long lattice piece to settle on top of the row of tartlets so that each tartlet is covered with lattice, carefully pulling the lattice so that it covers the tarts evenly. Using the tops of the metal tart rings as your cutting edge, gently press on the tart rings to trim the lattice tops to the size of each individual tartlet. You can now move the tartlets apart so they are evenly dispersed along the sheet pan.

2. Bake the tartlets for 25 to 30 minutes, until the top lattice crust browns and the filling puffs, bubbles, and browns slightly.

OPTION!

This tart makes a beautiful presentation for any number of fruits in season, especially peaches. Apples, pears, and cherries also work well and can be brown-buttered with ease. Substitute an equal amount of your favorite fruit and enjoy!

Blackberry BUCKLE PIE

MAKES 1
(9-INCH/23-CM) PIE

BUCKLE, BROWN BETTY, CRUMBLE, CRISP, COBBLER . . . what the hell is the difference? I'll tell you this much: A buckle is fruit baked into a single layer of cake, with a streusel-like topping. If you're me, you put it all in a pie shell. As for those others, well, let's just say they are tasty, no matter what their particular components.

FOR THE CRUST		
Simple Tart Dough (page 30)	½ batch	
FOR THE FILLING		
all-purpose flour	2 cups	250 g
baking powder	1 teaspoon	5 g
salt	1 teaspoon	6 g
unsalted butter	½ cup	115 g
brown sugar, firmly packed	1 cup	220 g
eggs	2	
buttermilk	½ cup	120 ml
juice and zest of 1 lemon		
vanilla bean paste	1 teaspoon	5 ml
blackberries	1 pint	340 g
FOR THE TOPPING		
unsalted butter, melted	1 cup	225 g
granulated sugar	½ cup	100 g
brown sugar, firmly packed	½ cup	110 g
salt	½ teaspoon	3 g
all-purpose flour	2½ cups	310 g

Procedure for the crust

1. Preheat the oven to 350°F (175°C). Roll the dough into a rough 11-inch (28-cm) round and line a 9-inch (23-cm) pie plate with it. Crimp the edges and dock the bottom of the dough. Freeze it for 20 minutes.

2. Line the crust with parchment, fill it with pie weights or dried beans, and bake it for 15 minutes. Remove the pie weights and parchment and bake for 10 minutes more, or until the raw-dough sheen is gone but the bottom of the crust hasn't browned. Set it aside.

Procedure for the filling

1. In a mixing bowl, whisk together the flour, baking powder, and salt.

2. In the bowl of an electric mixer fitted with the paddle attachment, cream together the butter and brown sugar until light and fluffy. Add the eggs, one at a time, beating well after each addition.

3. In a small bowl, whisk together the buttermilk, lemon juice and zest, and vanilla.

4. Add one-third of the flour mixture and then one-third of the buttermilk mixture to the butter and sugar. Beat until just combined. Continue alternating between the flour and buttermilk, making sure not to overmix. Gently fold in the blackberries by hand, using a large rubber spatula.

Procedure for the topping

In a large bowl, stir together the butter, both sugars, the salt, and the flour. Keep working the crumbs with your spoon or your fingers until the butter is absorbed and the mixture forms small clumps.

Assembly

Pour the filling into the prepared piecrust and smooth the top with a small offset spatula or the back of a spoon. Sprinkle the topping in an even layer over the filling and bake for 30 to 40 minutes, until the filling is set and springs back when you gently poke it.

Boysenberry TURN-OVERS

MAKES 12 TURNOVERS

OF ALL THE PLACES TO FIND THIS MOST DECADENT, BUT-TERY, SWEET, AND FRUITY OF DELICACIES, I'D NEVER HAVE THOUGHT IT WOULD BE A NATURAL-FOOD STORE TUCKED AWAY AT THE FOOT OF THE ROCKIES. But that's exactly where I got my first bite of the most delicious turnover I've ever eaten.

I spent a good chunk of my youth in Jackson Hole, Wyoming. For my mother, it was a getaway place that married the elevated grandeur of her native Alps with the laid-back calm of an all-American cowboy landscape. And although we looked to Jackson as a respite from everyday life, that didn't mean an escape from Mom's all-natural food regimen. She managed to find the one spot along the Teton Range that catered to all things flaxseed and tempeh, but—pastry hound that I am—I spied something in the front case that piqued my piehole's interest. It was a charming little triangle of pastry bliss, wearing the delicate stains of some luscious blue berry that was nestled inside but was so gloriously juicy that it wouldn't be contained and bubbled out to say hello. I wanted it. Badly.

This confection was a boysenberry turnover, or so said the sign. I persuaded my mother to purchase one, arguing that there could be nothing healthier than partaking of the native fruits. And what a fruit it was.

Traditional Puff Pastry (page 25)	¼ batch	
sugar	½ cup	100 g
Clearjel (see Note, page 57)	1 tablespoon	10 g
boysenberries	2 pints	680 g
juice and zest of 1 lemon		
egg wash (1 egg whisked with 2 tablespoons/30 ml water)		
unsalted butter, chilled and cut into tiny pieces	4 tablespoons	55 g
sanding sugar or turbinado sugar, for sprinkling	¼ cup	50 g

1. Preheat the oven to 375°F (190°C). Line a sheet pan with parchment. Roll the puff pastry into a very long strip, approximately 4 by 48 inches (10 by 122 cm). Let it rest for 15 minutes.

2. Meanwhile, in a small bowl, whisk together the sugar and Clearjel. In a mixing bowl, toss the berries with the lemon juice and zest. Sprinkle the sugar mixture over the fruit and toss until the berries are evenly coated.

3. With a very sharp knife, cut the dough strip into 12 (4-inch/10-cm) squares. Trim the sides so the edges are even and clean.

4. With a pastry brush, brush the edges of each dough square with the egg wash (this acts as the glue when you fold the dough to make the turnover).

5. Divide the filling evenly among the 12 pieces of dough, placing the filling in the middle of the square. Divide the butter evenly among the turnovers, dotting the top of the filling with the tiny pieces.

6. Fold each turnover in half to make a triangle. Seal the edges by gently pressing with your fingers.

7. Place the turnovers on the prepared sheet pan and brush each turnover with egg wash, then sprinkle with turbinado or sanding sugar.

8. Bake for 25 to 30 minutes, or until the pastries have puffed and are golden brown.

Gooseberry
FOOL
Tartlets

MAKES 8
(4-INCH/10-CM) TARTLETS

A FRUIT FOOL IS AN ENGLISH DESSERT THAT DATES BACK TO THE SIXTEENTH CENTURY. Like trifle, it's laden with cream. However, while a trifle consists of layers of elements, a fool requires that the fruit be gently folded into the whipped cream. The most common base for the fool is the gooseberry, an oval berry that comes in a tart green variety and a slightly sweeter pink one. As a dessert, fool is a lovely combination of tart, sweet, and creamy.

FOR THE PUREE		
fresh gooseberries (green or pink)	1 pound	455 g
granulated sugar	½ cup	100 g
salt	pinch	
FOR THE TART SHELLS		
all-purpose flour	1 cup, plus 2 tablespoons	125 g, plus 15 g
sugar	1 teaspoon	4 g
salt	pinch	
whole milk	½ cup	120 ml
unsalted butter	½ cup	115 g
eggs	5 (more or less)	
Traditional Puff Pastry (page 25)	½ pound	225 g
turbinado sugar, for sprinkling		
FOR THE ASSEMBLY		
heavy cream	¾ cup	180 ml
mascarpone cheese	¼ cup	60 g
confectioners' sugar	¼ cup	25 g
vanilla bean paste	1 teaspoon	5 ml

Procedure for the puree

1. Clean the berries of any stalks and stemmy bits. Reserve 8 whole berries to use as garnish and slice the remainder in half.

2. In a heavy-bottomed saucepan, heat the berries with the sugar and salt, stirring until the juices and the sugar begin to thicken. Transfer the mixture to a bowl and set it aside in the refrigerator to cool.

Procedure for the tart shells

1. Preheat the oven to 375°F (190°C). Then make a pâte à choux paste: In a mixing bowl, whisk together the flour, sugar, and salt. In a large saucepan over medium heat, bring the milk, ½ cup (120 ml) water, and the butter to a rolling boil.

2. Reduce the heat to medium low and add the flour mixture carefully but all at once. Immediately start stirring with a wooden spoon. Don't stop stirring until the mixture is smooth and comes together into a very thick paste that pulls away completely from the sides of the pan. This takes a few minutes.

3. Transfer the paste to the bowl of a stand mixer fitted with the paddle attachment. Mix on medium speed to cool the paste a bit. Add the eggs, one at a time, beating after each addition to make sure it's fully incorporated. There is a chance—based on relative humidity—that 5 eggs will be too many or too little. You want to form a thick paste that isn't runny but flows readily from a piping bag. Transfer the paste to a large pastry bag fitted with a large open tip. Set it aside.

4. Cut the puff pastry into 8 even pieces. Roll each into a rough 6-inch (15-cm) round and place it on a sheet pan lined with parchment paper. Dock the dough and refrigerate it for at least 20 minutes.

5. Line eight 4-inch (10-cm) individual fluted tart molds with the puff pastry, trimming away any excess dough. Brush the interior of the tart shells with the egg wash and then pipe the choux paste into the shells, filling them one-third of the way up. Using the back of a small teaspoon or a small offset spatula, spread the choux paste up the sides of each tart shell to create a little bowl. Sprinkle the interior of the shells with an even layer of turbinado sugar.

6. Bake the shells until the paste puffs into a flat dome and browns, about 45 minutes. Allow the shells to cool just until you can handle them and carefully slice off the top of each shell. If the interior is still a little moist, continue cutting off all the tops of the shells and pop the tops and bottoms back into the oven for 10 minutes to dry out a bit. Allow the shells to cool completely.

Assembly

1. In the bowl of an electric mixer fitted with the whisk attachment, beat the cream, mascarpone, and confectioners' sugar until you achieve stiff peaks (making sure not to overwhip the cream).

2. Transfer one-third of the whipped cream into a smaller bowl and gently stir it into the gooseberry puree, then gently fold the remaining whipped cream into the gooseberry mixture.

3. Divide the fool evenly among the shell bottoms, place a gooseberry on top of each, and cover gently with the tops.

STONE FRUIT

Schwarzwald TART

MAKES 1
(9-INCH/23-CM) TART

BLACK FOREST CAKE ISN'T NAMED FOR THE LOVELY SCHWARZWALD RANGE IN GERMANY, BUT RATHER BECAUSE IT INCLUDES THE AREA'S TRADITIONAL CHERRY BRANDY, KNOWN AS *KIRSCHWASSER*. So why not play with the lineup—the chocolate, the sour cherries, the whipped cream, and the *Kirschwasser*—and make a tart instead of a cake? Trust me, as long as it's got all of that good stuff, no one is going to complain.

FOR THE CRUST		
Chocolate Cookie Tart Crust (page 31)	1 batch	
FOR THE FILLING		
bittersweet chocolate, finely chopped	8 ounces	225 g
unsalted butter	½ cup	115 g
Kirschwasser (cherry brandy)	2 tablespoons	30 ml
eggs, separated	3	
salt	1 teaspoon	6 g
granulated sugar	½ cup	100 g
almond flour	3 ounces	85 g
FOR THE ASSEMBLY		
cherry preserves	2 tablespoons	30 ml
heavy cream	1 cup	240 ml
confectioners' sugar	¼ cup	25 g
vanilla bean paste	½ teaspoon	2.5 g
fresh cherries, whole	½ pound	225 g
egg white (optional)	1	
granulated sugar	¼ cup	50 g

Procedure for the crust

Preheat the oven to 350°F (175°C). Line a 9-inch (23-cm) round tart pan with the chocolate dough, dock the dough, and freeze it for 20 minutes. Line the dough with parchment and fill it with pie weights or dried beans. Bake the crust for 20 minutes, remove the pie weights and parchment, and set it aside.

Procedure for the filling

1. In a heatproof bowl set over a gently simmering pot of water, combine the chocolate, butter, and *Kirschwasser* and stir until melted. Keep warm.

2. In the bowl of a stand mixer fitted with the whisk attachment, whip the egg yolks until they are pale and thick and drip back into the bowl as a ribbon when you lift the whisk attachment from the yolks.

3. In the very clean bowl of a stand mixer fitted with a clean whisk attachment, whip the egg whites with the salt, then slowly add the sugar until you have soft, shiny white peaks. Do not overbeat to the point of stiff peaks; if you do, the tart will crack in the oven.

4. Fold the almond flour into the chocolate mixture until well combined. Gently add the beaten yolks and then fold in the egg whites.

Assembly

1. In a small bowl, gently warm the cherry preserves in the microwave at 50-percent power for 45 seconds. Brush the preserves over the bottom of the crust and then pile in the filling. Smooth the filling with a small offset spatula.

2. Bake the tart for 35 to 40 minutes, until the filling is set. Allow it to cool completely.

3. In a large bowl, whisk the cream, confectioners' sugar, and vanilla together until you achieve stiff peaks. Fill a pastry bag fitted with a large star tip with the whipped cream and pipe decorative filigree over the top of the tart.

4. With a clean pastry brush, paint each cherry with the egg white. Dip the cherry in the granulated sugar to cover the glazed portion. Place the sugar-coated cherries around the perimeter of the tart on top of the whipped cream. (If using raw egg white makes you squeamish, simply top the tart with the cherries as they are.)

AT THE END OF HER DAYS, MY MOTHER ONLY WANTED TO EAT TWO THINGS: SOLE MEUNIÈRE AND APRICOT TART. For weeks, I would make the quick trip across Key Bridge into Washington, D.C., and pick up an entire apricot tart from a sweet little French bakery tucked away in Georgetown. I could have made the tarts myself, but my utter sadness at watching my mother fade so quickly left me oddly unable to play with butter and sugar. But this tart was all that I could have wanted for my mother. The crust was tender with butter and ever so slightly sweet. The apricots were succulent but firm, a tart counterpoint to the rich crust they were nestled in. I bake this simple tart when I need to conjure the memory of my wonderful mother.

APRICOT TART

MAKES 1

(APPROXIMATELY 12-BY-16 INCH/ 30.5-BY-40.5 CM) TART

Sweet Tart Dough (page 30)	1 batch	
fresh or canned apricots	24 to 30	
sanding or turbinado sugar, for sprinkling	2 tablespoons	25 g

1. Preheat the oven to 350°F (175°C). Lightly coat a half sheet pan with nonstick spray.

2. Line the pan with the dough, gently pressing it up along the edges and making sure that the surface is relatively even. Dock the dough and place it in the refrigerator for at least 20 minutes.

3. Halve the apricots and discard the kernels. Line the dough with the apricots, cut sides up, then sprinkle the sanding or turbinado sugar over the fruit. (If using canned, lightly dry each apricot with a paper towel to sop up excess moisture.)

4. Bake the tart for 30 minutes, or until the dough starts to brown at the edges and the apricots become very tender.

OPTION!

Plum Tart!

Replace the apricots with either conventional plums or the beautiful Damsons (also known as Italian or prune plums) when they are in season.

THIS WAS A COVETED MORSEL AT MY BAKERY ON PIE DAY.
It's a simple cherry pie, but when cherries are in season and abundant,
there's nothing simple about the flavor. Just make sure you pit *all* of the
cherries. I don't think I need say more.

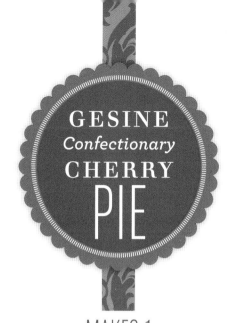

sugar	1 cup	200 g
ground cloves	pinch	
salt	pinch	
Clearjel (see Note, page 57)	3 tablespoons	30 g
fresh pitted cherries	7 cups	1.1 kg
juice and zest of 1 lemon		
All-Butter Easy Pie Dough (page 19)	1 batch	
Crust Dust (see Note, page 24) for the shell	1 to 2 tablespoons	10 to 20 g
unsalted butter, cubed into tiny pieces	3 tablespoons	42 g
egg wash (1 egg whisked with 2 tablespoons/30 ml water)		
sanding sugar or turbinado sugar, for sprinkling	2 tablespoons	25 g

GESINE
Confectionary
CHERRY
PIE

MAKES 1
(9-INCH/23-CM) DOUBLE-CRUST PIE

1. In a mixing bowl, whisk together the sugar, cloves, salt, and Clearjel. In a large bowl, toss the cherries with the lemon zest and juice until they are evenly coated. Sprinkle the sugar mixture over the cherries and again toss until evenly coated.

2. Divide the dough into 2 pieces, one slightly larger than the other. Roll the larger piece into a rough 11-inch (28-cm) round and line a 9-inch (23-cm) pie plate with it. Roll the second piece into a 9½- to 10-inch (24- to 25-cm) round. Cut out decorative shapes or lattice strips, or simply vent the round. Refrigerate both pieces until you are ready to proceed.

3. Preheat the oven to 350°F (175°C). Sprinkle the Crust Dust to cover the bottom crust, then pour in the cherry filling. Dot the top of the filling with the butter.

4. Cover the pie with whatever form of crust you have chosen for your top piece. Crimp the bottom and top crusts together at the edges. Brush the exposed dough with the egg wash. Sprinkle all over with sanding or turbinado sugar.

5. Bake the pie for 45 to 50 minutes, or until the filling is bubbling and the bottom and top crusts are golden brown.

CHERRY LAVENDER
Clafoutis

MAKES 1
(11-INCH/28-CM) TART

A CLAFOUTIS IS A FLANLIKE TART, HERE WITH CHERRIES SUSPENDED IN THE BAKED CUSTARD. Adding lavender allows for a subtle floral essence to come through without going so far as to taste of perfume. The tradition of this tart's native land, the Limousin region of France, maintains that the pits should remain in the cherries when baked in the tart. I'm going to ask—no, I'm going to *insist*—that you pit those cherries, because I know when I tuck into a tart, I'm going to bite down with relish, pit or no pit. And when given the options of going to the dentist or having another piece of tart, I'm going to choose the tart every time. So pit those cherries and have a second slice of pie.

cherries	1 pound	455 g
Sweet Tart Dough (page 30)	½ batch	
whole milk	¾ cup	180 ml
heavy cream	½ cup	120 ml
food-grade dried lavender (preferably organic)	1 ounce	30 g
all-purpose flour	2 tablespoons	15 g
granulated sugar	1 cup	200 g
salt	¼ teaspoon	1.5 g
vanilla bean paste	1 teaspoon	5 ml
eggs	3	
confectioners' sugar, for sprinkling	¼ cup	25 g

1. Preheat the oven to 350°F (175°C). Set aside a handful of especially pretty cherries, with stems, to use for decoration. Stem and cut the rest of the cherries in half, removing and discarding the pits; set the cherries aside.

2. Line an 11-inch (28-cm) tart pan with the dough, dock it, and freeze it for 20 minutes. Line the shell with parchment and fill it with pie weights or dried beans. Bake the shell for 20 minutes. Remove the pie weights and discard the parchment and bake for 5 minutes more, until the crust is golden.

3. In a large saucepan, simmer together the milk, cream, and lavender over low heat for 5 minutes. Remove the pan from the heat, let the mixture steep for at least 20 minutes to infuse the cream with lavender, then strain and return the cream to the saucepan.

4. In a mixing bowl, whisk together the flour, granulated sugar, salt, and vanilla. Whisk in the eggs until the mixture forms a smooth paste.

5. Simmer the cream over medium heat and then pour the hot liquid into the flour mixture in a steady stream, whisking constantly until combined. Set the bowl aside.

6. Raise the temperature of the oven to 375°F (190°C). Arrange the cherry halves evenly, cut sides down, on the tart shell.

7. Open the oven and set the crust on the pulled-out center rack. You are using this as your work surface because this next step is tricky. Gently, very gently, pour the cream mixture over the cherries. Gently push the rack back into the oven, close the door, and lower the temperature to 350°F (175°C). (You raised the temperature in the last step to make up for the heat lost while you had the oven door open.)

8. Bake the tart for 30 to 35 minutes, or until the custard is set. Cool it completely and dust it with confectioners' sugar. Arrange the reserved cherries around the perimeter.

YOU CAN'T SPEND A MOMENT OF SUMMERTIME IN BAVARIA WITHOUT CATCHING A GLIMPSE OF A *ZWETSCHGENDATS-CHI*, A RUSTIC TART MADE OF ITALIAN PRUNE PLUMS NESTLED IN A LOVELY CRUST. There are two ways of making this classic dessert: You can bake the plums in a sweet crust or in a yeasted crust. I've chosen to go with the latter here. Whichever you choose, you must use those dark-purple oval beauties when they are in season in the late summer.

Imperial
PLUM
TART
(Zwetschgen-datschi)

MAKES 1
(APPROXIMATELY 12-BY-16 INCH/ 30.5-BY-40.5 CM) TART

FOR THE CRUST		
bread flour	5 to 6 cups	700 to 840 g
instant yeast	1 tablespoon	12 g
salt	2 teaspoons	12 g
maple syrup	¼ cup	60 ml
eggs	2	
whole milk	1¾ cups	420 ml
zest of 1 lemon		
vanilla bean paste	1 tablespoon	15 ml
unsalted butter, at room temperature and cut into small pieces	4 tablespoons	55 g
FOR THE CRUMBLE		
unsalted butter, melted	1 cup	225 g
granulated sugar	½ cup	100 g
brown sugar, firmly packed	½ cup	110 g
salt	½ teaspoon	3 g
all-purpose flour	2½ cups	310 g
FOR THE ASSEMBLY		
Italian prune plums, in season, or traditional plums, cut in half lengthwise, pitted	2 pounds	910 g
whipped cream, for serving		

Procedure for the crust

1. In the bowl of an electric mixer fitted with the dough hook attachment, stir together 5 cups of the flour with the yeast and salt.

2. In a mixing bowl, whisk together the maple syrup, eggs, milk, lemon zest, and vanilla.

3. With the mixer on low, add the wet ingredients to the dry ones, and when they are just combined, slowly add the bits of butter.

4. Mix the dough until it starts to pull from the sides of the bowl and is very shiny. If the dough is still quite sticky, slowly add more flour from the remaining 1 cup (140 g). The mixing process can take quite a while, up to 15 minutes. Be patient.

5. Bulk proof the dough (see Note) in a large bowl sprayed with nonstick spray and covered with a damp kitchen towel, until the dough doubles in size, about 1 hour.

6. Punch down the dough, turn it onto a lightly floured surface, and roll it out into a rough 16-by-24-inch (40.5-by-61-cm) rectangle. Transfer it to a parchment-lined sheet pan and allow it to rest in the refrigerator for 20 minutes.

Procedure for the crumble

In a large bowl, stir together the butter, both sugars, the salt, and the flour. Keep working the crumbs with your spoon or your fingers until the butter is absorbed and the mixture forms small clumps.

Assembly

1. Preheat the oven to 350°F (175°C). Arrange the plums, cut sides up, in neat rows on the surface of the dough, then sprinkle the plums evenly with the crumble.

2. Bake the tart for 45 to 50 minutes, or until the dough is golden brown and baked through and the plums are tender. Serve it with freshly whipped cream.

NOTE

"Bulk proofing" simply means that the dough isn't yet formed into shape; it's simply being allowed to rise as a big blob.

APPLES
and
PEARS

I DIDN'T REALIZE HOW BEAUTIFUL AN APPLE PIE COULD BE UNTIL I COMBINED THE BUTTERY LUSCIOUSNESS OF A WELL-MADE PIECRUST WITH THE SWEET, CREAMY GOODNESS OF THESE LIGHTLY CARAMELIZED APPLES. By sautéing apples just slightly before baking, you minimize "crust bubble," that awkward empty space between the apple filling and the top crust that results when raw apples shrink to half their size in the heat of the oven. If you cook the apples ever so slightly before you assemble the pie, you preshrink them, which results in the perfectly packed slice—no bubble.

Not-So-Traditional

APPLE PIE

MAKES 1
(9-INCH/23-CM) DOUBLE-CRUST PIE

FOR THE CRUST		
Quick Puff Pastry (page 22)	¼ batch	
FOR THE FILLING		
large baking apples (see Note, page 85)	13	
zest and juice of 1 lemon		
all-purpose flour	3 tablespoons	22 g
brown sugar, firmly packed	1 cup	220 g
vanilla bean paste	1 teaspoon	2 g
cinnamon	1 teaspoon	3 g
salt	½ teaspoon	3 g
unsalted butter	2 tablespoons	28 g
heavy cream	¼ cup	60 ml
FOR THE ASSEMBLY		
Crust Dust (see Note, page 24)	1 to 2 tablespoons	10 to 20 g
egg wash (1 egg whisked with 2 tablespoons/30 ml water)		
sanding sugar or turbinado sugar, for sprinkling		

Procedure for the crust

1. Divide the dough into 2 pieces, one slightly larger than the other. Roll the larger portion into a rough 11-inch (28-cm) round. Line the bottom of a 9-inch (23-cm) pie pan with the dough, tuck the edges under and crimp them, then dock the bottom. Refrigerate the dough for 20 minutes.

2. Roll the second piece of dough into a rough rectangle, about ⅛ to ¼ inch (3 to 6 mm) thick. Using a 3-inch (7.5-cm) heart-shaped cookie cutter, cut out 16 heart shapes. Place them on a parchment-lined sheet pan and refrigerate them until needed.

Procedure for the filling

1. Peel, core, and cut the apples into slices ¼ inch (6 mm) thick. Toss the slices in a bowl with the lemon juice and zest to keep them from browning. In another bowl, whisk together the flour, brown sugar, cinnamon, and salt. Sprinkle this over the apples and toss until the fruit is evenly coated.

2. Melt the butter in a large heavy-bottomed pot. Add the apple mixture and sauté for 5 minutes. Add the cream and vanilla bean paste and continue to cook the apples, stirring often, until the juices thicken and the apples are just tender. Make sure not to overcook the apples or they will become mushy. Transfer the cooked apples to a large bowl and set them aside to cool completely.

Assembly

1. Preheat the oven to 350°F (175°C). Sprinkle the Crust Dust in an even layer on the bottom of the piecrust. Spoon the filling into the crust and top it with the hearts, placing them along the outer edge first, with the pointy ends facing inward (make sure the outer edge of the heart slightly overlaps the edge of the bottom crust—this takes about ten hearts). Create an inner, overlapping circle of hearts, using five more hearts, and place the last heart in the middle. The hearts should all overlap in such a way that you cannot see the filling.

2. Brush the egg wash over the top crust and sprinkle with sanding or turbinado sugar.

3. Bake for 45 minutes, or until the filling is bubbling and the top and bottom crusts are golden brown.

A NOTE FROM THE SWEETIE PIE

Selecting the correct apple for baking is crucial to your pie endeavors. The quality of a great baking apple is, first and foremost, taste. An apple that is sweet but possesses a pleasant amount of tart is best. Granny Smiths are the most commonly found baking apple; they are always available in large quantity, but they're often lacking in real apple flavor, and they are rarely as fresh as is best for apple pies, tarts, and galettes. The other qualities to look out for in apples are crispness and the ability to hold up to heat. The last thing anyone wants when cutting into a pie is the sight of fruit turned into indistinguishable mush (I'm talking to you, Red and Golden Delicious). My all-time favorite baking apples, available in the fall, are the brilliantly white-fleshed Cortland and the juicy Northern Spy. But keep your eye peeled for these baking beauties as well: Baldwin Tart, Jonagold, Rome Beauty, and Suncrisp. Mix and match apples for complexity of flavor.

APPLE
Tarte
TATIN

MAKES 1
(10-INCH/25-CM) TART

WHY IS IT THAT DESSERT LEGEND ALWAYS HAS THE FRENCH COMING UP WITH THE MOST MAGNIFICENT PASTRIES BY ACCIDENT? The Austrians create pastry to commemorate victory in battle; the Germans create pastry to get rid of leftovers; the English create desserts that can be simmered in one pot for days—but the French are always screwing up and coming up with something wonderful. What gives?

Tarte tatin is made up of not just *une* mistake *française* but *deux*! Puff pastry was allegedly created from an apprentice baker's blunder of forgetting to add butter to the dough. He ended up folding the butter in after the dough was mixed and—*voilà!*—laminated puff pastry. In the case of tarte tatin, the pastry idiots savants at the Hotel Tatin had meant to make a traditional apple tart with the apples baked in a tart shell. But someone left the apples caramelizing on the burner too long, so she thought she'd save the dessert by placing the pastry on top of the cooking apples. and then she shoved the entire thing in the oven to finish it off. In true French fashion, the disaster was delicious. Why doesn't this ever happen to me?

Traditional Puff Pastry (page 25)	8 ounces	225 g
tart apples, such as Granny Smith, cored, peeled, and cut into quarters (see Note, page 85)	10	
juice of 1 lemon		
unsalted butter	½ cup	115 g
vanilla bean paste	1 teaspoon	5 ml
brown sugar, firmly packed	1 cup	220 g
salt	¼ teaspoon	1.5 g
heavy cream, whipped, for serving	2 cups	480 ml

1. Roll the puff pastry into a rough 11-inch (28-cm) round, dock it, and refrigerate it for at least 20 minutes.

2. Toss the apples with the lemon juice. Set them aside.

3. In a 10-inch (25-cm) ovenproof skillet, melt the butter with the vanilla over low heat. Sprinkle this mixture with the brown sugar and salt. Continue to cook, stirring, until the sugar has melted.

4. Arrange the apples symmetrically in the skillet, spacing them as closely as possible so there are few gaps. You won't be able to fit all the apples in, but as they cook and their juices are released, they will shrink. Whenever you see gaps, add more slices of apple so that you are left with a packed layer of apples with little or no space between the pieces.

5. Cook until the sugar turns golden brown. This should take 25 to 30 minutes. Set the skillet aside to cool for 15 minutes.

6. Preheat the oven to 375°F (190°C). Place the round of puff pastry over the apples. Tuck in the excess dough around the edges, between the skillet and the apples.

7. Bake the tart for 30 minutes, or until the pastry has browned and is fully cooked through.

8. Allow the tart to cool for 10 to 15 minutes. The caramel syrup on the bottom of the pan needs time to set, but you do not want it to cool so much that the apples stick (if this happens, gently warm the pan over low heat on your stovetop to loosen them).

9. Invert a large serving plate on top of the skillet and flip the tart over to release it onto the plate. Don't burn yourself! Serve the tart with the whipped cream.

OPTIONS!

Option 1

Use quinces instead of apples! Or pears! Or even *mangoes*! If your fruit is firm enough, it will probably work very well in a tarte tatin.

Option 2

For individual tarte tatins, line a sheet pan with parchment and arrange 6 individual flan rings on top. Caramelize the fruit as instructed and divide the caramel syrup among the rings. Tightly pack the fruit into each ring in an even layer and top it with a round of puff pastry, tucking the edges in between the fruit and the ring before baking. Bake for 20 minutes, just long enough for the pastry to brown and puff.

German Apple Custard Tart

Apple Tarte Tatin

MY FIRST TASTE OF APPLE PIE WAS ACTUALLY THIS ONE—A GERMAN APPLE CUSTARD TART, WITH THE APPLES NESTLED IN A GORGEOUS BAKED CUSTARD. I can't take a bite of this stuff without remembering childhood, my beloved Omi, and the spanking I happily suffered for getting caught diving into the warm tart before dinner.

GERMAN
Apple Custard
TART

MAKES 1
(9-INCH/23-CM) SQUARE TART

FOR THE CRUST		
Sweet Tart Dough (page 30)	½ batch	
apricot preserves	1 tablespoon	15 ml
FOR THE FILLING		
unsalted butter	2 tablespoons	55 g
granulated sugar, divided	½ cup	100 g
zest and juice of ½ lemon		
rum	3 tablespoons	45 ml
apples, cored and sliced ¼ inch (6 mm) thick (see Note, page 85)	2	
heavy cream	1 cup	240 ml
vanilla bean paste	1 teaspoon	5 ml
salt	pinch	
eggs	2	
FOR THE ASSEMBLY		
confectioners' sugar	¼ cup	25 g
heavy cream	2 tablespoons	15 ml
slightly sweetened whipped cream, for serving		

Procedure for the crust

1. Preheat the oven to 350°F (175°C). Press the dough into a 9-inch (23-cm) square tart pan and freeze it for 20 minutes. Line the tart pan with parchment and fill it with pie weights or dried beans. Bake the crust for 15 minutes.

2. Remove the crust from the oven; remove the pie weights and parchment. Brush the crust with the apricot preserves and bake it for another 5 minutes. Set it aside.

Procedure for the filling

1. In a large saucepan, melt the butter along with ¼ cup (50 g) of the granulated sugar, the lemon zest and juice, and the rum. Add the apple

slices and sauté until just tender. Remove the apple slices with a slotted spoon, leaving the juices in the pan.

2. Add the cream, remaining granulated sugar, vanilla, and salt to the saucepan. Bring the mixture to a simmer.

3. In the meantime, whisk the eggs in a mixing bowl. Continuing to whisk, slowly pour the hot cream mixture in a steady stream into the eggs.

Assembly

1. Arrange the apple slices evenly on the crust, overlapping them slightly. Pour the custard over the apples. Carefully transfer the tart to the oven and bake it until the custard has set and the edges are slightly golden, 30 to 35 minutes.

2. In a small bowl, stir together the confectioners' sugar and the cream until smooth. Allow the tart to cool until only slightly warm. Using a pastry brush, gently brush the top of the apples with the sugar glaze. Allow the tart to cool completely, then carefully remove it from the tart pan and transfer it to a platter. Serve with slightly sweetened whipped cream.

THIS IS A GLORIOUS, TALL APPLE PIE! But it's possible to make any pie into a miniature beauty, or even a pie pop. This pie is particularly tasty because it contains the perfect combination—slightly tart Vermont apples laced with a touch of Vermont maple, topped with Vermont cheddar, and tucked into a flaky Vermont butter crust (at least I use Vermont butter). Whether you make it tiny or large, you get the perfect amount of each ingredient in each bite.

Vermont
APPLE
PIE

MAKES 1
(9-INCH/23-CM) PIE

FOR THE CRUST		
Quick Puff Pastry (page 22)	¼ batch	
FOR THE FILLING		
tart apples, like Vermont's Crispin	10	
Vermont maple sugar (if you can't find maple sugar, use brown sugar)	½ cup	110 g
all-purpose flour	4 teaspoons	10 g
salt	½ teaspoon	3 g
FOR THE ASSEMBLY		
finely shredded extra-sharp Vermont cheddar cheese	½ cup	60 g
egg wash (1 egg whisked with 2 tablespoons/30 ml water)		

Procedure for the crust

1. Divide the dough into two pieces, one piece slightly larger than the other. Roll the larger portion into a rough 11-inch (28-cm) round. Line the bottom of a 9-inch (23-cm) pie pan with the dough, leaving a slight overhang. Refrigerate for at least 20 minutes.

2. Roll the second, piece of dough into a 10-inch (25-cm) round (you want this to be slightly larger than a traditional top crust since it has to fit over the large mound of apples). Using a 1-inch round cutter (I use a small apple cookie cutter for the task), cut a vent hole in the middle of the dough. Cover the top crust dough with plastic wrap and refrigerate until needed.

Procedure for the filling

Core the apples and cut them into ½-inch to 1-inch (12- to 24-mm) cubes. Toss these in a bowl with the maple sugar, flour, and salt until evenly coated.

Assembly

1. Preheat the oven to 350°F (175°C). Sprinkle the Crust Dust in an even layer over the bottom crust. Pile the apples into the bottom crust, mounding them highest in the middle. Sprinkle the cheddar in an even layer over the apples. Place the top crust over the apples and crimp the bottom and top crust edges together.

2. Brush the top of the crust with the egg wash.

3. Bake for 45 minutes, or until the top crust is golden brown.

Almost every pie lends itself to being made miniature. You're limited only by the availability of the appropriate container. Not so with pie pops. Since they are free-form in nature, you can play with sizing willy-nilly (with some limitations), but you're better off when you use a filling that keeps its shape; runny fillings don't do well in the pop world. But that still leaves you with a ton of options: Wild Blueberry, Not-So-Traditional Apple, Vermont Apple, Gesine Confectionary Cherry.

The two tricks to making a beautiful and delicious pie pop are ensuring that your filling is thick enough to withstand being sandwiched between two layers of dough without the aid of a concave baking receptacle that would otherwise keep the filling in place, and working with a dough that holds its shape—I use the Part-Butter Easy Pie Dough (page 19). I also make sure that the pop is no smaller than 3 inches so that you're guaranteed of a decent filling-to-crust-ratio, and I use a stick that's sturdy enough to withstand the top-heavy weight of the pie. I like caramel-apple sticks best, but have been known to use wooden skewers and disposable chopsticks as well.

If I'm making simple **double-crusted** pie pops, I roll one batch of dough into a rough rectangle, about ⅛ inch thick, and cut 3-inch rounds from the dough, carefully rerolling scraps and letting the scraps rest for twenty minutes in the refrigerator before rolling out again. This will give you about forty pops, depending on how efficient you are about stamping out the rounds.

Allow the rounds to rest in the refrigerator for twenty minutes before assembling. Space the rounds a few inches apart on a parchment-lined sheet pan (remember, you're going to need extra space to give the sticks some room). Brush the bottom round with egg wash and place the stick onto the round of dough so that it's reaching halfway into the round. Press gently on the stick and place a table-spoon of filling on the middle of the round, on top of the small portion of stick that's lying on the dough. Place the second round of dough on top of the filling and, using the tines of a fork, gently press the edges together.

Personally, I like the top crust to be **latticed**. In this case, I divide the dough into two pieces, one slightly larger than the other. The large piece I roll into a rough rectangle and cut out twenty 3-inch rounds. For the other piece, I roll it into a rough ⅛-inch-thick rectangle to make into lattice. I use two types of lattice: The first is made with a handy tool called a lattice dough cutter (I use Ateco brand). It's a wheel with evenly spaced slicers that makes easy work of latticing. Make sure that your dough is nice and cool and that the top of the dough has a nice dusting of flour. Also dust the lattice roller with flour, as the dough tends to stick to the roller. Simply apply gentle but steady pressure on the roller and roll the cutter across the length of the dough. Continue until the entire rectangle has been latticed. I like to line up my bottom rounds with their sticks in place and then gently drape a large piece of lattice so that it covers multiple pops. I then use a 3-inch round cutter to stamp out the lattice so it fits perfectly over the bottom round and filling. To make this even easier, get your hands on a tool called a tart master (available at www.bakedeco.com). This tool cuts the lattice into a 3-inch round and also crimps the edges beautifully.

For a larger, tight lattice, cut the rectangle into ½-inch-long strips. On a parchment-lined sheet pan, weave the pieces so that there are no gaps in the dough to show the filling. You'll have a nice, large square of lattice. Refrigerate the lattice for twenty minutes and then stamp out 3-inch rounds (or heart shapes, as I have) and proceed as you would with a simple, round pie pop. Please visit www.pieitforwardcookbook.com for a video demonstration on making pie pops!

San's
APPLE
CRUMBLE

MAKES 1
(9-INCH/23-CM) PIE

VICTIMS OF OUR MOTHER'S TOTALITARIAN HEALTH-FOOD REGIMEN, WE MADE THE BEST OF IT ON TWENTY-SIXTH STREET, MY SISTER AND I. We had no access to sweets, zero acquaintance with McDonald's Happy Meals, and only a passing understanding of what joys bacon might bring to our culinary lives. So when our parents left us alone in the house for periods any longer than a half hour, Operation Sugar Deprivation went into immediate effect. We'd concoct and experiment, mashing together butter, sugar, and flour in any number of combinations, in the hope of creating something edible—or if not edible, at the very least sweet. Apple Crumble will forever be remembered as the pinnacle of our culinary scramble, and it's still a staple on our dessert menus.

FOR THE CRUST		
Quick Puff Pastry (page 22)	⅛ batch	
FOR THE CRUMBLE		
unsalted butter, melted	1 cup	225 g
granulated sugar	½ cup	100 g
brown sugar, firmly packed	½ cup	110 g
salt	½ teaspoon	3 g
all-purpose flour	2½ cups	310 g
FOR THE FILLING		
tart apples, peeled and cored and cut into ¼-inch (6-mm) slices (see Note, page 85)	5 to 6	
juice and zest of 1 lemon		
brown sugar, firmly packed	¼ cup	55 g
all-purpose flour	1 tablespoon	8 g
cinnamon	½ teaspoon	1.5 g

Procedure for the crust

1. Preheat the oven to 350°F (175°C). Roll the dough into a rough 11-inch (28-cm) round and use it to line a 9-inch (23-cm) pie pan. Dock the bottom of the crust, and freeze it for 20 minutes.

2. Line the crust with parchment and fill it with pie weights or dried beans. Bake it for 15 minutes. Remove the parchment and pie weights and bake it for about 10 minutes more—just until the raw-dough sheen is gone, but before there is any browning.

Procedure for the crumble

In a large bowl, stir together the butter, both sugars, salt, and flour. Keep working the crumbs with your spoon or your fingers until the butter is absorbed and the mixture forms clumps.

Procedure for the filling

In a large bowl, toss the apple slices in the lemon juice and zest. In another bowl, whisk together the brown sugar, flour, and cinnamon. Sprinkle the mixture on top of the apples and toss.

Assembly

1. Spoon the filling into the crust, then sprinkle the crumble in an even layer on top.

2. Bake the pie for 45 minutes, or until the fruit starts to bubble and the crumble is golden brown.

Poached
PEAR
TART

MAKES 1
(10-INCH/25-CM) TART

NOTE

If you don't have pistachio flour,
take blanched whole pistachios
and remove any remaining
skins. Pulse in a food processor
along with a few tablespoons of
sugar until you've created a fine
meal that is still dry. Take care
not to overprocess the mixture,
as it will turn into a paste.

POACHING PEARS IS A TIME-HONORED, AND DELICIOUS, WAY
TO ENJOY A GLORIOUS FRUIT. Poaching in a juicy red wine like a
Zinfandel or Malbec brings added depth of flavor. And the *color*! Oh,
the color is delightful, ruby red and glowing. As seen against the brightness of green pistachios, the color of the wine-saturated pear pops even
more spectacularly. And in my opinion, the combination of juicy and
sweet wine-infused pear mingling with the heady flavor of pistachio is
intoxicating.

FOR THE CRUST		
Sweet Tart Dough (page 30)	½ batch	
FOR THE POACHED PEARS		
red wine (on the fruit-forward side, such as Zinfandel or Malbec)	1 bottle	750 ml
sugar	1 cup	200 g
zest and juice of 1 lemon		
zest and juice of 1 orange		
nutmeg	½ teaspoon	1.5 g
firm pears (either Bosc or Anjou are fine), cored and cut into slices ¼ inch (6 mm) thick	6	
FOR THE FILLING		
pistachio flour (see Note)	½ cup	55 g
sugar	½ cup	100 g
egg yolks	6	
cornstarch	4 tablespoons	32 g
salt	pinch	
heavy cream	1 cup	240 ml
milk	1 cup	240 ml
FOR THE ASSEMBLY		
pistachio flour (see Note)	1 cup	110 g
cherry preserves	¼ cup	60 ml

Procedure for the crust

1. Preheat the oven to 350°F (175°C). Line a 10-inch (25-cm) tart pan with
    the dough, dock the bottom, and freeze it for 20 minutes.

2. Line the crust with parchment, fill it with pie weights or dried beans,
    and bake it for 15 minutes. Remove the pie weights and parchment from
    the crust and bake it for 10 minutes more, or until the bottom is cooked
    through and just beginning to brown. Set it aside to cool.

Procedure for the poached pears

1. In a large stockpot, combine the wine, sugar, zest and juice, and nutmeg. Stir continuously over medium heat until the sugar has completely melted.

2. Add the pear slices and simmer over medium heat until the pears are barely tender and still firm. Transfer the pear slices from the poaching liquid to a clean bowl using a small sieve or slotted spoon. Allow both the pears and the poaching liquid to cool completely. Return the pears to the poaching liquid and store them in the refrigerator overnight. This allows the color and flavor to seep into the pears more fully without overcooking them.

Procedure for the filling

1. In the bowl of an electric mixer fitted with the whisk attachment, whisk together the pistachio flour, sugar, egg yolks, cornstarch, and salt until light and fluffy.

2. In a heavy saucepan, bring the cream and milk to a simmer. With the mixer on low, carefully pour the hot milk mixture into the eggs. Continue beating until completely combined, scraping the bottom and sides of the bowl to ensure that all has been fully integrated.

3. Transfer the mixture back into the saucepan and continue to cook it over medium heat, whisking, until the mixture thickens to the consistency of mayonnaise. Transfer the pastry cream to a bowl and cover the top with plastic wrap laid directly on the surface to prevent a skin from forming. Refrigerate the pastry cream until needed.

Assembly

1. Stir the pastry cream gently to loosen it up, as it tends to firm up considerably in the refrigerator. (If it's still too chunky, transfer it to the bowl of an electric mixer fitted with the paddle attachment and beat it until it is smooth.) Spoon the pastry cream into the tart shell and smooth the top with the back of a spoon or a small offset spatula. Sprinkle the pistachio flour evenly over the tart. Refrigerate it for 1 hour, until firm. Arrange the pears in a fan pattern, starting at the center and working around, overlapping each layer so that the end effect is like that of an open flower.

2. In a small saucepan over low heat, warm the cherry preserves and water, stirring, until well combined. With a small pastry brush, paint the poached pear slices with the cherry preserve glaze. Serve immediately or refrigerate.

PEAR, WITH ITS SUBTLE SWEETNESS AND DELICATE FLA-
VOR, BLENDS EFFORTLESSLY WITH THE HERBACEOUSNESS
OF BOTH RHUBARB AND CARDAMOM. Add the delicious creami-
ness of vanilla-laced custard, and this tart will delight everyone's senses.

Simple Tart Dough (page 21)	½ batch	
rhubarb	6 stalks	
unsalted butter	1 tablespoon	14 g
sugar, divided	¾ cup	150 g
juice and zest of 1 lemon		
Bosc pear, cored and cut into wedges ¼ inch (6 mm) thick	1	
vanilla bean paste	1 teaspoon	5 ml
cardamom	¼ teaspoon	1 g
egg yolks	6	
heavy cream	2 cups	480 ml
sanding sugar or turbinado sugar, for sprinkling	¼ cup	50 g

MAKES 1
(9-INCH/23-CM) TART

1. Preheat the oven to 350°F (175°C). Line a 9-inch (23-cm) glass pie plate with the dough, dock the bottom of the crust, and freeze it for 20 minutes.

2. Line the crust with parchment and pie weights or dried beans and bake it for 20 minutes. Remove the weights and parchment and bake for 5 minutes more. Set aside.

3. Raise the oven temperature to 375°F (190°C). Cut the rhubarb stalks into ½-inch (12-mm) pieces. Melt the butter in a heavy-bottomed skillet, then add the rhubarb along with ¼ cup (50 g) of the sugar and the lemon juice. Sauté until the rhubarb is *just* tender. Add the pear slices and sauté for 2 minutes more. Spread the rhubarb and pears over the bottom of the piecrust.

4. In a mixing bowl, whisk together the vanilla, cardamom, lemon zest, egg yolks, remaining sugar, and cream until well combined. Pour this over the fruit and bake the pie for about 25 minutes, or until just set. Sprinkle it with turbinado sugar, and bake it for 10 minutes more.

A *PITHIVIER* IS THE ORIGINAL DOUBLE-CRUST PIE. Frankly it's the *best* double crust pie because what's better than luscious almond frangipane smooshed between two delectable rounds of puff pastry? Still thinking about that? That's right! Nothing!

FOR THE CRUST		
Traditional Puff Pastry (page 25)	¼ batch	
FOR THE FRANGIPANE FILLING		
almond paste	5 ounces	140 g
unsalted butter	3 tablespoons	42 g
all-purpose flour	2 tablespoons	15 g
egg	1	
pear, cored and thinly sliced	1	
egg wash (1 egg whisked with 2 tablespoons/30 ml water)		

PEAR FRANGIPANE *Pithivier*

MAKES 1
(10-INCH/25-CM) PASTRY

Procedure for the crust

1. Preheat the oven to 375°F (190°C). Line a sheet pan with parchment.

2. Divide the puff pastry in half and roll each piece into a 10-inch (25-cm) round approximately ⅛ inch (3 mm) thick. Refrigerate for 20 minutes.

Procedure for the filling

Place the almond paste in a food processor and pulse until the paste is broken apart. Add the butter, flour, and egg, and process until smooth.

Assembly

1. Place the first round of dough on the prepared sheet pan. Brush the edge of the dough with the egg wash and mound the frangipane on top, leaving a 1-inch (2.5-cm) border all around. Fan the pear slices on top of the frangipane.

2. Place the second round over the first and press down on the edges so that they adhere.

3. Using a sharp knife, cut the edges of the pastry to create a fluted edge.

4. Pierce the center of the pastry to create a steam hole and then, using the same sharp knife, score the pastry, starting at the steam hole and gently etching a curved line to the edge of the pastry. Repeat this curve evenly around the pastry.

5. Bake for 20 to 25 minutes, until the pastry has puffed and is a deep golden brown.

Springerle PEAR TART

MAKES 1
(9-INCH/23-CM)
DOUBLE-CRUSTED PIE

SPRINGERLE ARE EMBOSSED COOKIES LACED WITH EXTRACT OF ANISE, THAT HERB SLIGHTLY REDOLENT OF LICORICE. Springerle is the name of both the cookies and of the molds from which they are made. Springerle were a staple in my childhood home during the Christmas season, and for years I wondered why this beautiful technique was relegated to the holidays. Then it occurred to me that I am a pastry chef. I can play with my springerle molds and anise extract whenever and however I want! So I present to you the springerle pear tart. It's got all the flavor and a big dose of beauty, and it's available to you any time of the year.

FOR THE CRUST		
Sweet Tart Dough (page 30), anise option	½ batch	
Part-Butter/Part-Shortening Pie Dough (page 19)	½ batch	
cornstarch, for rolling		
FOR THE FILLING		
pears, cored and cut into slices ¼ inch (6 mm) thick (see Note, page 106)	8	
Zante currants	½ cup	72 g
chopped walnuts	½ cup	60 g
orange zest	1 teaspoon	2 g
orange juice	2 tablespoons	30 ml
anise extract	½ teaspoon	2.5 ml
brown sugar, firmly packed	½ cup	110 g
all-purpose flour	2 tablespoons	15 g
salt	½ teaspoon	3 g
unsalted butter	2 tablespoons	28 g
heavy cream	¼ cup	60 ml
FOR THE ASSEMBLY		
Crust Dust (see Note, page 24)	2 tablespoons	20 g
egg wash (1 egg whisked with 2 tablespoons/30 ml water)		

Procedure for the crust

1. To make the bottom crust, line a 9-inch (23-cm) pie plate with the sweet dough, dock the bottom of the dough, and refrigerate it.

2. To make the top crust, roll the pie dough into a rough 9-inch (23-cm) round, using a traditional rolling pin. Liberally dust the top of the dough with cornstarch. Using a springerle rolling pin that has been generously

sprinkled with cornstarch, roll the patterned pin along one half of the dough, applying even pressure to ensure that the pattern transfers. Dust the pin again and continue rolling down on the second half until the top of the dough is completely embossed. (Springerle block molds can be used in place of a patterned rolling pin.)

3. Allow the top crust to dry out a bit, uncovered, in a cool, dry place—not in the refrigerator, because there is too much moisture there. In order for the design to bake into the crust, the dough has to dry just enough before baking for the pattern to set.

Procedure for the filling

1. Toss the pears, currants, and walnuts with the orange zest and juice and the anise extract. In a mixing bowl, whisk together the brown sugar, flour, and salt. Sprinkle this over the pear mixture and toss until the pears are evenly coated.

2. Melt the butter in a very large saucepan. Add the fruit-and-nut mixture and sauté for 5 minutes. Add the cream and continue to sauté until the pears are just tender and the sauce thickens, 10 to 15 minutes. Transfer the filling to a large bowl and refrigerate it until it's completely cool.

Assembly

1. Preheat the oven to 350°F (175°C). Sprinkle the bottom piecrust with an even layer of Crust Dust, and spoon in the pear filling. Carefully transfer the top crust, laying it gently on the filling and crimping the edges of the bottom and top crusts together decoratively.

2. Brush the top crust gently with the egg wash. Bake for 45 to 50 minutes, or until the top and bottom crusts are golden brown.

A NOTE FROM THE SWEETIE PIE

Keep in mind that pears need to be firm for baking. I always choose those that aren't completely ripe to ensure that they'll hold together. For poaching—see, for example, the red-wine-poached pears in the tart on page 98—I use Bosc pears. Other varieties that hold up well to baking are Anjou and Bartlett. Comice pears are delicious but best enjoyed raw. Just remember that a soft pear is the one you want to eat raw; a firm pear is best for poaching or baking.

DATES
and
FIGS!

Oatmeal
DATE
TURNOVERS

MAKES 18
INDIVIDUAL TURNOVERS

THERE'S SOMETHING ABOUT THIS LITTLE TART THAT BRINGS TO MIND AN AFTER-SCHOOL SNACK. It's sweet yet deliciously wholesome. It's also hearty enough to tide you over until supper. Just don't ruin your dinner; it's easy to eat one too many of these little gems.

FOR THE FILLING		
pitted dates, chopped	½ pound	225 g
brewed coffee	1 cup	240 ml
lemon zest	1 teaspoon	2 g
cinnamon	1 teaspoon	3 g
salt	pinch	
FOR THE CRUSTS		
unsalted butter	½ cup	115 g
vegetable shortening	¼ cup	50 g
brown sugar, firmly packed	1 cup	220 g
egg	1	
salt	pinch	
whole milk	¼ cup	60 ml
vanilla bean paste	1 teaspoon	5 ml
all-purpose flour	2 cups	250 g
baking soda	1 teaspoon	5 g
salt	1 teaspoon	6 g
quick-cooking oats	2 cups	160 g
FOR THE ASSEMBLY		
egg wash (1 egg whisked with 2 tablespoons/30 ml water)		

Procedure for the filling

In a heavy-bottomed saucepan over medium heat, bring the dates, coffee, lemon zest, cinnamon, and salt to a simmer, stirring frequently until the mixture thickens to a jammy consistency, about 10 minutes. Allow to cool to room temperature.

Procedure for the crusts

1. In the bowl of an electric mixer fitted with the paddle attachment, cream the butter, shortening, and brown sugar until light and fluffy. Add the egg and beat until it's fully incorporated. Mix in the milk and vanilla.

2. In a large bowl, whisk together the flour, baking soda, and salt. Slowly add this mixture to the batter until just combined. Fold in the oats by hand. Turn the dough out onto a large sheet of plastic wrap, seal it up, and refrigerate it for at least 30 minutes. The dough will be very soft until it is chilled.

Assembly

1. Preheat the oven to 350°F (175°C). Line two sheet pans with parchment.

2. Dust a work surface with flour. Roll the dough to ⅛ inch (3 mm) thick and, with a biscuit cutter or round cookie cutter, cut into 18 (4-inch/10-cm) rounds. Place the rounds on the prepared sheet pans, spacing them 1 inch (2.5 cm) apart.

3. Brush the edges of each round with the egg wash.

4. Place 1 tablespoon (15 ml) of filling on one half of each dough round. Fold the dough over the filling and press the edges together. Score the tops of the turnovers decoratively and bake them for 15 minutes, or until golden brown.

STICKY
Toffee Pudding
TART

MAKES 1
(9-INCH/23-CM) TART

TRADITIONALLY, STICKY TOFFEE PUDDING IS A STEAMED SPONGE CAKE MADE WITH DATES AND THEN SOAKED IN TOFFEE SYRUP. *Who needs tradition, though, when you can mix it up and make a tart with an equal measure of moist goodness and stickiness along with the convenience of a pastry shell?*

FOR THE CRUST		
Simple Tart Dough (page 21)	1 batch	
FOR THE FILLING		
all-purpose flour	1 cup	125 g
baking powder	1 teaspoon	5 g
salt	1 teaspoon	6 g
pitted dates	1 cup	152 g
hot brewed coffee	1 cup	240 ml
baking soda	1 teaspoon	5 g
unsalted butter, softened	4 tablespoons	55 g
dark brown sugar, firmly packed	¾ cup	165 g
eggs, lightly beaten	2	
lemon zest	1 teaspoon	2 g
vanilla bean paste	1 tablespoon	15 ml
FOR THE SAUCE		
unsalted butter	½ cup	115 g
heavy cream	½ cup	120 ml
dark brown sugar, firmly packed	1 cup	220 g
salt	pinch	

Procedure for the crust

Preheat the oven to 350°F (175°C). Roll the dough into a rough 11-inch (28-cm) round. Line a 9-inch (23-cm) round or square tart pan with the dough and dock. Freeze the dough for 20 minutes. Line the dough with parchment, fill it with pie weights or dried beans, and blind bake it for 20 minutes. Remove the weights and parchment and bake the crust for 10 to 15 minutes more, until the bottom no longer looks raw and wet.

Procedure for the filling

1. In a small bowl, whisk together the flour, baking powder, and salt. Set aside.

2. Chop the dates into very small pieces. Place them in a small bowl and add the hot coffee and baking soda and stir. Set aside until cooled.

3. In the bowl of an electric mixer fitted with the paddle attachment, beat the butter and brown sugar until light and fluffy. Add the eggs one at a time and then the lemon zest and vanilla; beat until blended. Gradually add the flour mixture and mix until just combined.

4. Remove the mixing bowl from the machine and fold in the date mixture by hand, using a rubber spatula. Pour the filling into the prepared shell. Bake until the pudding is set, 30 to 35 minutes.

Procedure for the sauce

Combine the butter, cream, brown sugar, and salt in a heavy-bottomed saucepan over medium-low heat. Stir constantly until the sugar has completely melted, then raise the heat to medium and simmer gently until the sauce thickens, about 10 minutes.

Assembly

Spread 1 cup (240 ml) of the sauce over the top of the tart. Serve it immediately, drizzling a little more toffee sauce over each piece.

THE DELICACY OF HONEY-LACED PASTRY CREAM AND THE HEARTY JUICINESS OF SWEET FIGS BRING TO MIND THE GLORY THAT MUST HAVE BEEN THE DESSERT COURSE OF A GRECIAN BANQUET. Fresh figs have the added benefit of being simply gorgeous when split open.

Fresh
FIG
TART

MAKES 1
(9-INCH/23-CM) TART

FOR THE CRUST		
Sweet Tart Dough (page 30)	½ batch	
FOR THE FILLING		
buttermilk	½ cup	120 ml
heavy cream	½ cup	120 ml
honey	¼ cup	60 ml
egg yolks	3	
cornstarch	2 tablespoons	16 g
zest of 1 lemon		
salt	pinch	
FOR THE ASSEMBLY		
fresh mission figs, cut in half	15	

Procedure for the crust

1. Preheat the oven to 350°F (175°C). Line a 9-inch (23-cm) tart pan with the dough, dock the bottom, and freeze for 20 minutes.

2. Line the crust with parchment and fill with pie weights. Bake for 15 minutes. Remove the pie weights and parchment and bake the crust for 15 to 20 minutes more, or just until it is golden brown and baked through.

Procedure for the filling

In a heavy-bottomed saucepan over medium heat, bring the buttermilk and cream to a simmer. In the bowl of an electric mixer fitted with the whisk attachment, beat the honey, egg yolks, cornstarch, zest, and salt at medium-low speed until smooth and fluffy. Slowly add the simmering buttermilk mixture to the honey mixture and beat at medium-low speed until smooth. Transfer the mixture back to the saucepan and whisk it over medium heat until it thickens to the consistency of mayonnaise. Spoon into a bowl and cover with plastic wrap placed directly on the surface of the cream. Refrigerate until completely cool.

Assembly

To assemble the tart, spoon the pastry cream into the tart shell, smoothing with an offset spatula. Arrange the figs right side up, on top of the pastry cream. Serve immediately.

FIGGY POPS

MAKES 16
(3-INCH/12-CM) INDIVIDUAL POPS

I SPEND FAR TOO MUCH FREE TIME RUMINATING OVER THE ORIGINS OF FOOD. For instance, I have sat still, in what must have seemed a high yogic trance, wondering at the invention of such miraculous foodstuffs as bread. Who in the h-e-double-hockey-sticks decided it would be a taste sensation to take a festering bacteria (yeast) and mash it up with grain? And for that matter, who first husked, hulled, and ground wild wheat? And don't get me started on figs! They are one of agriculture's big finds. It's perhaps the first plant to be actively cultivated for human consumption. Three fossilized figs were found in a Neolithic village, dating back to 9400–9200 BC, a prehistoric Whitman's Sampler in the making if ever there was one.

With a lovesick Fred Flintstone in mind, I bring you Figgy Pops, a lightly sweet and tender crust encasing a filling of gorgeous, ancient sweetness. Assemble a few Figgy Pops as an edible bouquet for your sweetheart; I promise they work better than ye olde club to the head and subsequent drag into your cave.

FOR THE CRUSTS		
all-purpose flour	2 cups	250 g
sugar	½ cup	100 g
salt	1 teaspoon	6 g
zest and juice of 1 lemon		
unsalted butter, very cold, cut into small pieces	¾ cup	170 g
vegetable shortening, chilled in the freezer for 5 minutes	4 tablespoons	50 g
eggs	2	
vanilla extract	1 teaspoon	5 ml
FOR THE FILLING		
dried figs, diced	1 cup	150 g
sugar	¼ cup	50 g
salt	pinch	
vanilla extract	1 teaspoon	5 ml
FOR THE ASSEMBLY		
egg wash (1 egg whisked with 2 tablespoons/30 ml water)		
SPECIAL EQUIPMENT		
wooden caramel apple sticks	16	

Procedure for the crusts

1. In the bowl of a food processor, pulse together the flour, sugar, salt, and lemon zest. Add the butter and shortening and pulse until the mixture resembles coarse cornmeal. Whisk together the eggs, lemon juice, and vanilla. Continue pulsing and add the egg mixture.

2. Turn the dough out onto a lightly floured work surface and work it gently with your hands, pressing it into a loose disk while incorporating any dry, floury spots into the dough. Cover the dough with plastic wrap and chill it overnight.

Procedure for the filling

1. In a small saucepan over medium-low heat, combine the figs, sugar, salt, and vanilla with ½ cup (120 ml) water. Let the mixture simmer, stirring constantly, until it thickens.

2. Transfer the fig mixture to a bowl, cover it with plastic wrap, and allow it to cool in the refrigerator overnight.

Assembly

1. Preheat the oven to 350°F (175°C) and line two baking sheets with parchment. Roll out the dough to a little over ⅛ inch (3 mm) thick. Using a biscuit cutter or a 3-inch (7.5-cm) round cookie cutter, cut 32 rounds from the dough. (If you have fewer, it's okay, but you do need an even number of rounds.) You can reroll the scraps, but be gentle so you don't overwork the dough.

2. Arrange half of the rounds on the baking sheets. Brush them with the egg wash and place a caramel apple stick onto the round (the top third of the stick should sit on the dough and the rest will lie on the sheet pan). Dollop 1 tablespoon (15 ml) of filling onto the middle of each round.

3. Place the remaining dough rounds over the filling and, using the tines of a fork, gently press down on the edges to seal the pop. Gently brush the top of each pop with egg wash.

4. Bake for 15 to 20 minutes, or just until the pastry has browned.

SWEET

and

CREAMY

MY COUSIN BARBARA AND I TOOK MY BELOVED HUSBAND, RAY, UP MY FAVORITE MOUNTAIN ONE SUMMER. My great affection for Hochfelln springs from several factors: First, the lovely mountain is plunked right in the middle of the beautiful town where my German family lives. Second, the vista from the top is incomparable and gives you a full view of neighboring towns' church spires and abundant green forests. Third, there are *two* fabulous restaurants there, one halfway up the mountain and another at the tippy-top.

At the halfway mark, we stopped in at the sweet café nestled beside the cow fields and sat at a picnic bench with a few slabs of cake and some beer. Ray asked what our neighboring diners were drinking—it looked curiously like melted milkshake. I explained that it was buttermilk. Ray was horrified. But it was true—and quite normal.

This refreshment has failed to catch on in the States, but in our own South, where the other half of my family lives, buttermilk is indeed a staple ingredient of many dishes, most of them desserts. I've added fresh peaches here to leave no doubt that this is an all-American buttermilk creation. So while I'm not counting on you to replace your Gatorade with buttermilk, I am confident that you'll make this pie and enjoy it on a glorious summer day while sitting on a picnic bench of your choosing.

Buttermilk
PEACH
PIE

MAKES 1
(9-INCH/23-CM) PIE

FOR THE CRUST		
Quick Puff Pastry (page 22)	⅛ batch	
FOR THE FILLING		
light brown sugar, firmly packed	2 cups	440 g
all-purpose flour	¼ cup	30 g
salt	¼ teaspoon	1.5 g
nutmeg	¼ teaspoon	1 g
buttermilk	1½ cups	360 ml
unsalted butter, melted and cooled	½ cup	115 g
zest and juice of 1 lemon		
vanilla extract	1 teaspoon	5 ml
eggs	3	
FOR THE TOPPING		
fresh peach, cut into slices ¼ inch (6 mm) thick	1	
heavy cream	1 cup	240 ml
confectioners' sugar	¼ cup	25 g
vanilla bean paste	1 teaspoon	5 ml

Procedure for the crust

1. Preheat the oven to 350°F (175°C). Roll the dough into a loose 11-inch (28-cm) round and let it rest for 20 minutes in the refrigerator.

2. Transfer the dough to a 9-inch (23-cm) glass pie plate. Dock the bottom and decoratively crimp the edges of the crust. Chill for another 20 minutes.

3. Line the crust with parchment and pour in pie weights or dried beans to fill it to the very top. Bake for 20 minutes, remove the weights and parchment, and set the crust aside.

Procedure for the filling

1. Raise the oven temperature to 400°F (205°C). In a mixing bowl, stir together the brown sugar, flour, salt, and nutmeg. In another bowl, mix together the buttermilk, butter, lemon zest and juice, and vanilla.

2. In the bowl of an electric mixer fitted with the whisk attachment, whisk the eggs. Slowly add half of the dry mixture and then add the liquid. Add the remaining half of the dry mixture and continue mixing until the contents are completely incorporated. Do not let the mixture get foamy.

3. Pour the filling into the crust and bake for 15 minutes. Reduce the oven to 350°F (175°C) and continue baking until the filling is set, about 40 minutes. Allow the pie to cool completely.

Assembly

1. Fan out the peach slices around the edge of the cooled pie.

2. In the bowl of an electric mixer fitted with the whisk attachment, beat the cream, confectioners' sugar, and vanilla until you achieve stiff peaks. Take care not to overbeat the whipped cream. Pipe the whipped cream in a decorative manner onto the middle of the pie.

MAPLE, WHEN BADLY TREATED, CAN BE A CLOYING MESS IN PASTRY—AND THAT'S A WASTE OF PERFECTLY GORGEOUS AMBER NECTAR. But it doesn't have to be that way. If you are judicious about adding New England's liquid pride, you will be rewarded with a gorgeous pie of unparalleled tastiness and just the right amount of sweetness. By brûléeing the top of the pie, you add crispiness that acts as a wonderful counterpoint to the smooth creaminess of the filling. It elevates the entire tart into a work of mapley art.

Brûléed
MAPLE
Custard
TART

MAKES 1
(8-inch/20-cm) tart

FOR THE CRUST		
Simple Tart Dough (page 21)	½ batch	
FOR THE FILLING		
cornstarch	¼ cup	32 g
grade-B maple syrup (see Note, page 120)	½ cup	120 ml
heavy cream	2 cups	480 ml
whole eggs	2	
egg yolks	2	
vanilla bean paste	1 teaspoon 5 ml	
salt	½ teaspoon	3 g
nutmeg	¼ teaspoon	1 g
FOR THE BRÛLÉE TOPPING		
granulated sugar	½ cup	100 g

Procedure for the crust

1. Preheat the oven to 350°F (175°C). Line an 8-inch (20-cm) fluted tart pan with a removable bottom with the dough. Dock the bottom of the dough and freeze it for 20 minutes.

2. Bake the crust for 15 minutes. Set it aside to cool.

Procedure for the filling

1. In a large metal bowl, whisk together the cornstarch and maple syrup. Add the cream, eggs and yolks, vanilla, salt, and nutmeg, and whisk until combined.

2. Bring a large saucepan of water to a simmer. Place the metal bowl over the water and whisk constantly until the mixture thickens. Immediately pour the custard through a fine sieve directly into the tart shell.

3. Bake the tart for 20 minutes, or until the custard is set. Allow it to cool completely, at least 4 hours.

Procedure for the brûlée topping

1. Make sure the custard has no moisture beading on the top. If it does, take a paper towel and gently dab away the liquid. Take care not to ding the custard.

2. Sprinkle the sugar evenly over the top of the custard—use all of it, shimmying it around to create an even coating.

3. Using a kitchen torch with the flame on medium-high to high, melt the sugar; hold the flame about 1½ inches (4 cm) away from the surface of the custard, keeping it in constant motion over the sugared area. You'll see the sugar start to liquefy and bead. Keep waving the flame over the sugar, never allowing the heat to stay in one spot for an extended period of time. Keep at it until the sugar has caramelized and the entire surface of the custard turns a medium amber. Do not use a broiler to caramelize the sugar as that will melt the custard.

A NOTE FROM THE SWEETIE PIE

Why getting a B is better than an A

Just because your maple syrup is stamped with an "A" and proclaims itself to be "fancy" doesn't mean that it's the best Vermont nectar out there. We here in the green mountains go for the dark brew, the syrup that's graded with a "B," because it packs a muskier, heartier maple flavor. If you want to stick with the fancy on your waffles, feel free. But for baking, when flavors can be lost and jumbled in the heat of your stovetop or oven, the more flavorful B will hold on to its maple goodness to the very end (and it's cheaper).

I ONCE ANSWERED A CALL TO OUR BAKERY THAT ENDED UP TAKING A VERY STRANGE TURN. The gentleman on the other end of the line asked, "Do you make cream pies?" Proud of my legion of offerings, I said, "Of course!"

"Well, what kind?" he asked rather breathlessly.

"All kinds! Banana, coconut, strawberry, chocolate, caramel . . ."

"But are they *cream* pies? You're not saying they are *cream* pies."

"Uh, okay. Banana *cream* pie. Coconut *cream* pie . . ."

As I prattled on and on, the other end of the line became disturbingly quiet. It took me far too long to figure out that the strange man had no interest in actually ordering a pie.

Which is too bad, actually, because they are delicious little confections and require a single base recipe upon which you can create thousands of options. Just call me—I'll go through the list for you.

Vanilla CREAM PIE

MAKES 1
(9-INCH/23-CM) PIE

FOR THE CRUST		
Quick Puff Pastry (page 22)	⅛ batch	
FOR THE ASSEMBLY		
Pastry Cream (page 35), made with 1 tablespoon (15 ml) vanilla bean paste added during step 1, chilled	1 batch	
heavy cream	1 cup	240 ml

A NOTE FROM THE SWEETIE PIE

Pastry cream stiffens considerably when cooled, so to get it beautifully smooth and spreadable, transfer to a mixing bowl and whisk until smooth.

Procedure for the crust

1. Preheat the oven to 350°F (175°C). Roll the dough into a rough 11-inch (28-cm) round. Line a 9-inch (23-cm) pie plate with the dough, crimp the edges decoratively, dock the bottom, and freeze for 20 minutes.

2. Line the crust with parchment, fill it with pie weights or dried beans, and bake it for 15 minutes. Remove the weights and parchment and bake the crust for 20 minutes more, or until it is golden brown and baked through. Set it aside to cool completely.

Assembly

1. Stir the cooled pastry cream (which will have stiffened as it chilled) with a wooden spoon until it loosens and becomes smooth. Place about three-quarters of the pastry cream into the prepared crust.

2. Whip the cream to stiff peaks and fold it into the remaining pastry cream. Transfer the mixture to a pastry bag fitted with a large star tip and pipe the whipped cream mixture decoratively over the filled pie.

Simple Custard
FRUIT
TART

MAKES 1
(9-INCH/23-CM) TART

YES, IT'S SIMPLE. It's a tart made up of a crust, pastry cream, and fruit. But if you take the time to cut your fruits just so and then arrange them carefully and artfully, alternating colors and showcasing fruits in season and at the height of their flavor and beauty, you'll offer your guests a glorious feast not only for their mouths, but for their eyes as well.

FOR THE CRUST	1 CUP	240 ML
Quick Puff Pastry (page 22)	¼ batch	
FOR THE FILLING		
Pastry Cream (page 35), made with 1 tablespoon (15 ml) vanilla bean paste added during step 1	1 batch	
kiwis	2	
strawberries	1 pint	340 g
raspberries	1 pint	340 g
blueberries	1 pint	340 g
red currants	1 bunch	
cherries	1 handful	
FOR THE ASSEMBLY		
Fruit Glaze (page 37)	1 batch	
heavy cream	1 cup	(240 ml)

Procedure for the crust

1. Preheat the oven to 350°F (175°C). Roll the dough into a rough 11-inch (28-cm) round or square. Line a 9-inch (23-cm) pie plate or tart tin with the dough, crimp the edges decoratively (if using a pie plate) or trim the excess (if using a tart tin), and dock the bottom. Freeze the crust for 20 minutes.

2. Line the crust with parchment and fill it with pie weights or dried beans. Bake it for 15 minutes. Remove the weights and parchment and bake the crust for 20 minutes more, or until it is golden brown and baked through. Set it aside to cool completely.

Procedure for the filling

Prepare the pastry cream as instructed on page 35, adding the vanilla during the first step, when you combine the milk and cream.

Procedure for the fruit

1. Peel the kiwis and slice them into rounds ⅛ inch (3 mm) thick; if desired, use a small heart-shaped cookie cutter to cut the rounds into hearts.

2. Hull the strawberries, slice them in half, and, using a petit-four cutter or small cookie cutter, stamp them into heart shapes. Wash the raspberries, blueberries, currants, and cherries, and remove any stems or leaves (except for the cherries—leave the stems on and you can leave them unpitted). Pat the fruit dry with a paper towel and set it aside.

Assembly

1. Prepare the fruit glaze as instructed on page 37, transfer it to a small bowl, and set it aside.

2. Whip the cream until you achieve stiff peaks. Remove the pastry cream from the fridge. It will probably be quite stiff, so take a wooden spoon and stir until it loosens and becomes smooth. Gently fold the whipped cream into the pastry cream until you see no more white streaks. Transfer the lightened pastry cream to the prepared crust, smoothing the surface with a small offset spatula.

3. Arrange the fruit decoratively across the top of the pastry cream. Use a pastry brush to spread the apricot glaze gently onto the fruit to create a lasting glaze. Serve the tart immediately or refrigerate it for up to 1 day before serving.

A NOTE FROM THE SWEETIE PIE

Pastry cream should be used within two days of making it. But there is an exception: You can bake with it for up to a week. Usually you make your pastry cream on the stovetop, let it cool, and then immediately pile it into your pie shell, lightened or unlightened. Since it's made with eggs and cream, the shelf life of the stuff isn't long. But if you suddenly remember that you've got a half batch of pastry cream left over in the fridge a week later, you can add some to your apple-pie filling before baking for a deliriously decadent custardy pie. Or mix some pumpkin puree into the pastry cream and divide it among little squares of puff pastry to make pumpkin turnovers. Don't throw the stuff away! Instead, invent new ways to use leftover pastry cream by baking with it.

BOSTON CREAM PIE ISN'T A PIE—IT'S A CAKE. We all know this, and yet we've never bothered to correct the misnomer. Rumor has it that the delicious cake got its name from the fact that the layers were originally baked in pie plates. So I've taken the name literally and made a pie that's also a cake—the name now fits, but you still get what you've come to know and love. Quite frankly, there's something quite decadent about combining the two, a cakelike filling and a delicious tender crust.

Boston
CREAM
PIE

MAKES 1
(9-INCH/23-CM) PIE

FOR THE CRUST		
Simple Tart Dough (page 21)	½ batch	
FOR THE CAKE FILLING		
sugar	½ cup	100 g
unsalted butter	½ cup	115 g
egg	1	
vanilla extract	1 teaspoon	5 ml
all-purpose flour	1 cup	125 g
salt	1 teaspoon	6 g
baking powder	1 teaspoon	5 g
buttermilk	½ cup	120 ml
FOR THE CREAM FILLING		
sugar	¼ cup	50 g
cornstarch	2 tablespoons	16 g
egg yolks	3	
vanilla bean paste	1 teaspoon	5 ml
milk	½ cup	120 ml
heavy cream	½ cup	120 ml
FOR THE GLAZE		
unsalted butter	2 tablespoons	28 g
heavy cream	¾ cup	177 ml
corn syrup (optional)	1 tablespoon	15 ml
salt	pinch	
bittersweet chocolate, finely chopped	8 ounces	225 g

Procedure for the crust

Preheat the oven to 350°F (175°C). Line a 9-inch (23-cm) pie plate with the dough and freeze it for 20 minutes. Line the crust with parchment paper, fill it with pie weights or dried beans, and bake it for 15 minutes. Set it aside.

Procedure for the cake filling

1. In the bowl of an electric mixer fitted with the paddle attachment, cream together the sugar and butter until light and fluffy. Add the egg and vanilla and beat until fully incorporated.

2. In another bowl, whisk together the flour, salt, and baking powder. Add half of the flour mixture to the sugar mixture and mix. Add half of the buttermilk and mix. Add the remaining flour and then the buttermilk, mixing after each addition. Mix until just incorporated. Pour the batter into the crust and bake for 1 hour, until the cake springs back when you touch it. Allow it to cool completely.

Procedure for the cream filling

1. In the bowl of an electric mixer fitted with the whisk attachment, whisk the sugar, cornstarch, egg yolks, and vanilla until light and fluffy.

2. In a heavy saucepan, simmer the milk and cream. Pour the milk mixture in a steady stream into the egg-yolk mixture with the mixer on medium-low speed. When all the milk is added, increase the speed to high. Stop the mixer, scrape down the bottom and sides of the bowl, and resume whisking on high until the mixture is smooth.

3. Transfer the custard back into the saucepan and cook over medium heat, whisking constantly, until it thickens to the consistency of mayonnaise. Transfer the pastry cream to a bowl and cover the top with plastic wrap laid directly on the surface, to prevent the formation of a skin. Refrigerate the pastry cream until it is completely cool.

Procedure for the glaze

Place the chocolate in a large mixing bowl. Combine the butter, cream, corn syrup, and salt in a saucepan and heat until the mixture just comes to a simmer. Pour the simmering cream mixture over the chocolate and wait for a few minutes. Whisk the mixture until the glaze has emulsified and is smooth and shiny. Keep this warm and pliable until you use it. If it hardens, heat the mixing bowl over a pot of simmering water, stirring occasionally, until the glaze is workable again.

Assembly

1. Spoon the pastry cream over the top of the cooled cake and, using a small offset spatula, smooth it in an even layer to the very edges.

2. Carefully pour the glaze on top of the pastry cream and, with a clean offset spatula, smooth it so that it covers the pastry cream completely. Serve the pie immediately or refrigerate it for up to a day before serving.

GÂTEAU
ST. HONORÉ

MAKES 1
(11-INCH/28-CM) TART

SAINT HONORÉ IS THE PATRON SAINT OF BAKERS. To celebrate him, the French broke out their big guns and shoved all their specialties into one tart because, as you well know, more is more. And that means it's better. So get ready for puff pastry, choux rings and puffs, pastry cream, heavy cream, and caramel all in one place. You'll be thanking Saint Honoré for being such a stellar patron as to have deserved such a sweet pastry namesake.

FOR THE BASE		
Traditional Puff Pastry (page 25)	⅛ batch	
FOR THE CHOUX PASTE		
milk	½ cup	120 ml
unsalted butter	4 tablespoons	55 g
all-purpose flour	1 cup	125 g
sugar	1 teaspoon	4 g
salt	½ teaspoon	3 g
eggs	5 (more or less)	
FOR THE FILLING AND ASSEMBLY		
Pastry Cream (page 35), prepared with just a pinch of salt	1 batch	
heavy cream	1 cup	240 ml
Clear Caramel for Glazing (page 36)	1 batch	

Procedure for the base

Roll the dough into an 11-inch (28-cm) round. Refrigerate it for at least 30 minutes.

Procedure for the choux paste

1. As you make the choux, remember, this is the stuff cream-puff and éclair shells are made of, so it's going to look like a paste, not like a traditional cake batter or dough! In a large saucepan, combine the milk, butter, and ½ cup (120 ml) water and bring the mixture to a simmer over medium heat.

2. In a mixing bowl, whisk together the flour, sugar, and salt. When the milk mixture reaches a vigorous simmer, dump the flour mixture into the pan all at once. Immediately begin stirring with a wooden spoon and continue with this until the mixture thickens to a paste and dries out enough that it pulls away from the sides of the pan.

3. Transfer the paste to the bowl of an electric mixer fitted with the paddle attachment. Mix it for a minute to allow some of the steam to escape. Add the eggs, one at a time, mixing after each addition to make sure the egg is fully incorporated. Continue to add eggs until a smooth, thick paste is formed that isn't runny but will flow readily from a piping bag. Depending upon the on relative humidity, you may need more or less than 5 eggs.

4. Transfer the paste to a large pastry bag fitted with a large open tip and refrigerate it until needed.

Assembly

1. Prepare the pastry cream according to the directions on page 35, reducing the amount of salt to a pinch. Keep chilled until ready to use.

2. Preheat the oven to 375°F (190°C). Transfer the puff pastry round onto a parchment-lined sheet pan. Dock the dough. Pipe 4 concentric choux circles, each about ½ inch (12 mm) thick, on the pastry round, starting at the outermost edge and finishing in the middle (space them a little bit apart). Pipe half-dollar-sized dollops of choux directly on the space remaining on the sheet pan to create the little cream puffs you'll be attaching to the edges of the pastry later. Bake until both the choux and pastry are puffed and golden brown. Set them aside to cool completely (do not refrigerate, as this will make the pastry soggy).

3. In a large bowl, with a hand whisk, whip the cream into stiff peaks. Stir the chilled pastry cream with a wooden spoon until it loosens and becomes smooth. Fold half of the pastry cream into the whipped cream until there are no white streaks left. Transfer this lightened pastry cream to a large pastry bag fitted with a medium/small open tip.

4. Poke small holes in the bottom of the choux puffs. Insert the open tip into the holes and fill them with the lightened pastry cream. Set these filled profiteroles aside on a sheet pan and refrigerate them, along with the remaining lightened pastry cream.

5. Gently spoon the unlightened pastry cream on top of the choux rings, spreading it to the edges. Refrigerate for at least 1 hour, until the pastry cream has set.

6. Shortly before you are ready to assemble the dessert, make the caramel as described in the recipe on page 36. Allow the caramel to cool for 5 minutes and then carefully dip the tops of the cream puffs in the caramel. Set them aside to allow the glaze to harden.

7. Once the caramel coating has hardened, dip the bottoms of the cream puffs into the liquid caramel to create an adhesive. (If the caramel in the pot has hardened, gently reheat it over low heat until it flows easily again, being careful not to burn it.) Place them along the choux ring at the edge of the pastry round. Pipe the remaining lightened pastry cream into the middle of the cake in a decorative manner (there is a specific pastry tip called the St. Honoré that is traditionally used to decorate this cake, but any beautiful piping will do).

8. Dip the ends of a sugar whisk (a ball whisk with the top cut off—see Note) in the leftover caramel, or coat a small spoon with caramel, then move the whisk or spoon around the perimeter of the St. Honoré, spinning sugar on top of the cream puffs. Serve the pie immediately.

OPTION!

A Paris-Brest is a cream-puff dessert made with hazelnut-praline pastry cream and chopped hazelnuts. You can flavor the pastry cream in the St. Honoré with ¼ cup (60 ml) hazelnut-praline paste, added just as the cream begins to thicken on the stovetop so that it melts and is incorporated perfectly. To finish, sprinkle chopped hazelnuts on top of the caramel to add a little nutty flavor!

A NOTE FROM THE SWEETIE PIE

To make the thin, hard strands of caramel that decorate the perimeter of the Gateau St. Honoré, I use a piece of homemade equipment I call a "sugar whisk." You can buy a specialized piece of equipment at pastry supply stores for hundreds of dollars, or you can buy a $5 ball whisk, get a pair of wire cutters, and cut off the top of the whisk (those pieces of wire that arch over), so that you're left with independent wire tines. Clip the tines as evenly as possible. You dip the tines into the hot sugar and are rewarded with multiple strands of gorgeous sugar!

YIN-YANG
Cheesecake

MAKES 1
(8-INCH/20-CM) CHEESECAKE

IT MIGHT SOUND CRAZY, THIS COMBINATION OF GREEN TEA (OR MATCHA) AND MANGO, BUT THEY COMPLEMENT EACH OTHER BEAUTIFULLY. The green tea adds an earthy counterpoint to the tropical sweetness of the mango. And the colors! Any doubts you have about the pairing will flee when you see the two married on your plate.

Sweet Tart Dough (page 30), Matcha option	½ batch	
cream cheese	2 (8-ounce) packages	2 (225-g) packages
soft chèvre (goat cheese)	1½ pounds	680 g
sugar	1½ cups	300 g
eggs	4	
egg yolks	2	
all-purpose flour	2 tablespoons	15 g
salt	½ teaspoon	3 g
zest and juice of 1 lemon		
matcha (green tea powder)	4 tablespoons	12 g
mango puree	½ cup	120 ml
green food coloring	scant drop	
orange food coloring	scant drop	

1. Preheat the oven to 325°F (165°C). Set aside 1 tablespoon (15 ml) of dough (wrap it in plastic wrap and refrigerate). Pat the remainder of the dough into an 8-inch (20-cm) cake ring set upon a sheet pan lined with parchment paper or a springform pan that's been liberally coated with nonstick cooking spray. You can also use, as I have, a yin/yang mold (available online at Amazon.com and cake-supply shops). If you do, remove the S-shaped piece from the middle for this stage and proceed as you would with a regular cake ring.

2. Bake the crust for 20 minutes, or until it is ever-so-slightly golden brown. Set it aside while you make the cheesecake batter. Reduce the oven temperature to 275°F (135°C).

3. In the bowl of a stand mixer fitted with the paddle attachment, beat the cream cheese, chèvre, and sugar until smooth. Add the eggs and yolks one at a time. Scrape down the sides of the bowl and beat until the eggs and the cream cheese are fully incorporated. Add the flour, salt, lemon zest and juice, and beat until just combined.

A NOTE FROM THE SWEETIE PIE

Cheesecakes crack from time to time. It's just the danger of working with such deliciousness. But there are ways to avoid crackage. The first is to use a water bath. That's a method wherein you bake the cheesecake surrounded by a wall of warm water. This regulates the heat beautifully within the baking cheesecake and prevents the possibility of fissures. However, you need a water-tight baking vessel for this to work. The vessel most often used to bake cheese-cakes is a springform, and there are myriad ways for water to seep into the seams. Common practice is to surround the springform with aluminum foil, but you're still courting damp cheesecake. I choose to bake it at a low heat in a cake ring. Cake rings are bottomless, so a water bath is completely out; low heat's the only option. Once the cheesecake is set, with a slight wobble in the center, turn the heat in the oven off, open the door slightly to let the heat escape, and allow the cheesecake to cool slowly in the oven. Cooling too quickly can shock the batter and cause cracks. This takes an awfully long time—hours—but the results are absolutely worth it.

4. Pour the batter through a fine sieve into a large bowl. Transfer half of the batter to a separate bowl and stir in the green tea powder.

5. Add the mango puree to the plain batter, and stir until it is completely incorporated.

6. If you're using the yin-yang mold, put the S piece back into the middle of the mold. Press down gently so that it touches the crust but doesn't slice all the way through to the bottom. Pour the mango batter into one side of the mold, very carefully. You may have more batter than you need. If so, don't try to force it into the mold; otherwise, it will seep into the matcha side. Gently smooth the top of the cake with a small off-set spatula. Pour the green tea batter into the other side, being careful not to spill over onto the mango side. Smooth the surface with a clean, small offset spatula. If you are using a plain cake ring or springform, first pour the green tea batter into the cake form, on top of the prepared crust. Then gently pour the mango on top of the green tea layer to form two separate cheesecake layers. The green tea batter will be thicker and can withstand the mango layer's weight.

7. Bake the cheesecake for 15 minutes, then reduce the heat to 225°F (110°C) and continue baking for 1 to 1½ hours more, until the cake has set. The cheesecake should never brown or crack. If you get a hint of browning, open the oven door to allow excess heat to escape quickly and reduce the heat to 200°F (90°C).

8. When the cheesecake stops wiggling when tapped, turn off the heat and allow it to sit in the oven overnight (to cool it too quickly in the fridge will invite cracking). Refrigerate it for 1 hour before serving.

9. While the cheesecake cools, take out the remaining crust dough and divide it in half. Dye one piece green (a scant drop of green food coloring is sufficient) and one half orange (again, a scant drop of food coloring will do). It's best to wear latex gloves when coloring the dough, gently kneading each piece until the color is evenly distributed. Refrigerate the dough for 10 minutes and then roll it out on a lightly floured surface to about ¼-inch thick. Cut a small round of each, about ½ inch in size, and place on a parchment-lined sheet pan. Bake at 325°F for 5 minutes, just until the edges start to brown slightly. Allow to cool completely and then place the green round on the fattest portion of the mango cheesecake, and the orange round on the fattest portion of the matcha cheesecake.

CAN YOU SAY "DESPERATION" PIE? This is the pie that happens when there's nothing else around to fill a waiting crust. It's also known as Hoosier Pie, Indiana Pie, Quaker Pie, and Finger Pie. In Amish country, replace the sugar with molasses to make Shoofly Pie. In my part of the world, where we sugar the maples, the tradition is to use maple syrup.

The list of ingredients is beautifully small and adaptable. Any way you sugar it or fill it, this pie is as simple as can be and hits the spot when you have little else in the pantry and quiet pie desperation takes hold.

Simple Tart Dough (page 21)	½ batch	
granulated sugar	1 cup	200 g
dark brown sugar, firmly packed	¼ cup	55 g
cornstarch	¼ cup	32 g
salt	½ teaspoon	3 g
heavy cream	1 cup	240 ml
whole milk	1 cup	240 ml
vanilla bean paste	1 teaspoon	5 ml
unsalted butter, cut into very small pieces	2 tablespoons	28 g
nutmeg	¼ teaspoon	1 g

MAKES 1
(9-INCH/23-CM) PIE

1. Preheat the oven to 350°F (175°C). To make the crust, line a 9-inch (23-cm) tart pan with the dough and freeze it for 20 minutes. Line the crust with parchment, fill it with pie weights or dried beans, and bake it for 15 minutes. Remove the parchment and pie weights and bake the crust for 5 more minutes, or until the bottom loses its raw-dough sheen.

2. Meanwhile, in a mixing bowl, whisk together both sugars, the cornstarch, and the salt. Pour the mixture into a heavy saucepan, add the cream, milk, and vanilla, and whisk over medium-low heat until the sugar has melted. Increase the heat to medium high, continuously stirring, until the mixture thickens. Pour the filling into the prepared piecrust. Dot the top with the butter and then sprinkle it with nutmeg. Bake the pie for 40 to 45 minutes, or until it is set and golden brown.

OPTION!

For Shoofly Pie, reduce the granulated sugar by ½ cup (100 g) and replace with ½ cup (120 ml) of molasses; for Maple Sugar Pie, replace all the dark brown sugar and ¼ cup (50 g) of granulated sugar with ½ cup (120 ml) maple syrup. Then proceed as you would with the Sugar Cream Pie procedure.

Apricot QUARK TART

MAKES 1
(10-INCH/25-CM) TART

THERE IS A RAGING DEBATE ABOUT WHAT'S BETTER: a New York–style cheesecake with its super dense, cream-cheese filling, or the lighter, fluffier European version that's usually made with quark (in Germany) or ricotta (in Italy). Why do we have to argue? Why can't we all just get along? It's *cheese*, for goodness' sake—it's all good in my book.

Sweet Tart Dough (page 30), Lemon citrus option	1 batch	
eggs, separated	4	
sugar	½ cup	100 g
zest and juice of 1 lemon		
whole milk	3 tablespoons	45 ml
vanilla bean paste	½ teaspoon	2.5 ml
quark or farmer's cheese	1 pound	455 g
flour	1 tablespoon	8 g
salt	½ teaspoon	3 g
fresh or canned apricots, cut in half and pitted	7 to 8	

1. Preheat the oven to 325°F (165°C). Use the dough to line the bottom and sides of a 10-inch (25-cm) cake ring set on a parchment-lined sheet pan or a springform pan coated with nonstick spray. Dock the bottom of the dough and freeze it for 20 minutes.

2. Line the dough with parchment, fill it with pie weights or dried beans, and bake it for 15 minutes. Remove the pie weights and parchment and bake the crust for 5 to 10 minutes more, or just until the bottom loses its raw-dough sheen. Leave the oven on.

3. Meanwhile, in the bowl of a stand mixer fitted with the whisk attachment, whisk together the egg yolks, sugar, lemon zest and juice, milk, and vanilla until the mixture thickens and lightens slightly.

4. Take the bowl from the mixer and add the quark, using a large rubber spatula or wooden spoon to gently fold it together with the egg-yolk mixture until just combined. Sift the flour over the batter and gently fold it in.

5. In a separate metal bowl, whisk together the egg whites and the salt until stiff peaks form, being careful not to beat so much that the whites begin to dry and clump. Gently fold the egg whites into the batter until no white streaks remain.

6. Line the bottom of the crust with the apricots, cut sides up. Pack them tightly. Pour the batter on top of the apricots and shimmy the pan to settle the mixture into the crevices between the apricots and to pop any air bubbles.

7. Bake at 325°F (165°C) for 1 to 1½ hours, or until set. The middle of the filling will still wiggle ever so slightly, and that's good. Leave the tart in the oven, but turn off the heat. Prop the door open so that it cools slowly.

8. Once the cake is cool enough to handle, release it from the pan by running a thin, sharp knife around the edge. Chill it in the refrigerator for at least 1 hour before serving.

Earl Grey
TRUFFLE
TART

MAKES 1
(9-INCH/23-CM) TART

EARL GREY TEA WAS ACTUALLY NAMED FOR THE SECOND EARL GREY, WHO WAS BRITISH PRIME MINISTER IN THE 1830S. As prime minister, he received gifts from the world over, including a black tea blended with the heady bergamot citrus. He continued to enjoy the brew, allegedly having it custom blended to suit his very particular tastes. The mousse that fills this tart is blended exactly to my specifications, pleasing my very American palate while infusing my treat with a global sophistication every girl enjoys flirting with, and it certainly doesn't hurt that there are Earl Grey–infused truffles on each slice.

FOR THE CRUST		
Sweet Tart Dough (page 30)	1 batch	
FOR THE FILLING		
Earl Grey tea bags	2	
unflavored gelatin	1 generous tablespoon	generous 7 g
sugar	1 cup	200 g
egg whites	5	
salt	pinch	
heavy cream	1½ cups	360 ml
mascarpone cheese	½ cup	115 g
vanilla bean paste	1 teaspoon	5 ml
FOR THE TRUFFLES:		
Earl Grey tea bags	2	
heavy cream	¾ cup	177 ml
unsalted butter	2 tablespoons	28 g
bittersweet chocolate, chopped	8 ounces	225 g
cocoa powder, for dusting		

Procedure for the crust

1. Preheat the oven to 350°F (175°C). Line a 9-inch (23-cm) tart pan with the dough, dock it, and freeze it for 20 minutes.

2. Line the crust with parchment and fill it with pie weights or dried beans. Bake it for 15 minutes. Remove the parchment and pie weights and bake the crust for 15 minutes more, or until the bottom begins to brown and is baked through. Set it aside to cool completely.

Procedure for the filling

1. Bring ¼ cups (300 ml) water to a boil. Place the tea bags in a glass measure, pour the water over the bags, and allow them to steep until the tea cools slightly.

2. In a microwave-safe bowl, add the gelatin and pour ¼ cup (60 ml) of the brewed Earl Grey over it, making sure that each particle of gelatin is saturated, looking a bit like wet sand. (If there are dry particles peeking through when you microwave the gelatin, you'll scorch it.) Microwave on 50-percent power for 30 seconds at a time, swirling the bowl after each session, until the gelatin is completely melted. Be careful not to over-heat the gelatin because this can kill its efficacy.

3. Gently reheat the remaining tea if it's cooled too much (touch a bit to your wrist and if it feels cold, you'll need to reheat—like checking a baby's formula) and stir in the melted gelatin. You want to time this so that the mixture will still be liquid when you incorporate it into the whipped cream in step 7; you'll end up with chunks of gelatin if it is starting to seize when it hits the cold whipped cream. Basically, it needs to cool enough that it won't melt the whipping cream or meringue when added, but it must not set. Set the mixture aside while you make the meringue.

4. In a heavy saucepan, combine the sugar and ⅓ cup (75 ml) water. Stir the mixture over low heat until the sugar has completely dissolved. Clip on a candy thermometer, stop stirring, and heat the syrup to 234°F (112°C).

5. Meanwhile, in the bowl of a stand mixer fitted with the whisk attachment, whisk the egg whites with the salt on high until foamy. When the sugar syrup reaches temperature, lower the speed of the mixer to medium and carefully pour the syrup down the side of the bowl. Return the speed to high and whip until the meringue is shiny and bright white and maintains a stiff peak when you lift the whisk attachment from the meringue. Transfer it to a metal bowl and set it aside.

6. To the same mixer bowl in which you whisked the egg whites (you don't have to clean it), add the cream, mascarpone, and vanilla and whip until you've achieved soft peaks. Gently fold the whipped cream into this meringue.

7. Now you're ready to complete the filling. Check your gelatin mixture. It should be fluid and somewhere between lukewarm and room temperature. Quickly add the gelatin mixture to the meringue/cream mixture and fold it until just combined. Work swiftly to ensure a smooth, silken texture. Spoon the mousse into the crust and smooth it with a small offset spatula, mounding it higher toward the middle. Refrigerate the pie until the filling has set, at least 2 hours.

Procedure for the truffles

1. In a heavy saucepan, steep the tea bags in the cream and butter for at least 3 minutes, keeping the heat to medium so that the cream doesn't boil over.

2. When the cream is saturated with the tea color, remove the mixture from the heat; carefully extract the tea bags, squeezing any excess moisture back into the pan. Add the chocolate and allow the pan to sit undisturbed for a minute. Whisk until the mixture is smooth and all the chocolate has melted. Transfer the ganache to a bowl and cover it with plastic wrap. Refrigerate until it sets, at least 2 hours.

3. Pour some cocoa powder into a flat dish. Using a melon scoop, a teaspoon-size cookie scoop, or a spoon, scoop out 1 rounded teaspoon (5 ml) of ganache. Roll the ganache in your hands to create a uniform ball and then coat it with cocoa. It's messy, so wearing a pair of latex gloves helps a great deal. Refrigerate until set, about 20 minutes.

Assembly

Arrange the truffles on top of the tarts. Serve immediately.

WHEN I WAS A KID, WE'D OFTEN SPEND OUR SUMMERS IN GERMANY WITH FAMILY. Once we got there, though, all eyes turned to Italy. Because once it starts to get warm, the Germans I know pack up their socks and sandals and head south for some *dolce vita*. The trip meant I got to indulge in two of my favorite desserts: *affogato*, which is espresso poured over vanilla gelato, and tiramisu. This tart pays homage to my childhood fixation with sugar and coffee—with more than enough added chocolate to please anyone.

ESPRESSO TART

MAKES 1
(9-INCH/23-CM) TART

FOR THE CRUST		
Sweet Tart Dough (page 30), Espresso option	½ batch	
FOR THE FILLING		
heavy cream	1 cup	240 ml
whole milk	½ cup	120 ml
instant espresso powder	1 teaspoon	1 g
vanilla bean paste	1 teaspoon	5 ml
sea salt	½ teaspoon	3 g
high-quality bittersweet or semisweet chocolate	10 ounces	280 g
egg	1	
FOR THE ASSEMBLY		
heavy cream	1 cup	240 ml
mascarpone cheese	¼ cup	60 g
confectioners' sugar	¼ cup	25 g
brewed espresso, cooled (or 1 teaspoon/5 ml coffee extract or 1 tablespoon/3 g espresso powder dissolved in 1 tablespoon/15 ml hot water)	2 tablespoons	30 ml
high-quality cocoa powder, like Valrhona or Callebaut, for sprinkling		
chocolate-covered espresso beans, for garnish		

Procedure for the crust

Preheat the oven to 350°F (175°C). Line a 9-inch (23-cm) tart pan with the dough, dock it, and freeze it for 20 minutes. Line the crust with parchment and fill it with pie weights or dried beans. Bake it for 15 minutes. Remove the weights and parchment and bake for 5 minutes more, or until the bottom of the crust loses its raw-dough sheen.

Procedure for the filling

1. Heat the cream, milk, espresso powder, vanilla, and salt in a saucepan over medium heat until the mixture just begins to simmer. Remove the pan from the heat and add the chocolate. Allow everything to stand undisturbed for a few minutes, then whisk until the chocolate is completely incorporated and the mixture is smooth.

2. In a small bowl, lightly beat the egg. Add about ¼ cup (60 ml) of the chocolate mixture to the egg, whisking constantly to prevent scrambling. Pour the egg-chocolate mixture into the larger chocolate portion, still whisking constantly, until the egg is incorporated and the mixture begins to thicken.

3. Pour the chocolate into the crust and bake it for 30 minutes, or until the outer edges are set but the middle of the tart still has a little bit of wiggle (not a jiggle, not a full-out runny-batter shimmy, but a nice wobble, as you'd look for in a cheesecake). Allow the tart to cool completely.

Assembly

1. In the bowl of an electric mixer fitted with the whisk attachment, whisk together the cream, mascarpone, confectioners' sugar, and espresso until you achieve stiff peaks.

2. Transfer the whipped cream to a pastry bag fitted with a large star tip and pipe it decoratively around the edges of the tart. Sift cocoa on top and add chocolate-covered beans for a little caffeinated flourish.

A NOTE FROM THE SWEETIE PIE

I've been asked on more than one occasion whether espresso or coffee can be left out of a recipe. On the one hand, yes, coffee is rarely an integral or chemically required component. It's most often used as a flavor enhancer, unless you are making a dessert whose very essence is coffee. You'll see coffee in chocolate recipes, since it heightens and complements chocolate. If you hate coffee, if your palate is so refined that you can discern the molecular components within each bite and will be offended beyond the pale that the caffeinated (or decaf . . . you can use that too) beverage has made an appearance on your fork, by all means leave it out. But if you have a taste for adventure, keep it in.

Butterscotch Meringue Pie

Espresso Tart

Velvet Elvis Pie

Velvet
ELVIS
PIE

MAKES 1
(9-INCH/23-CM) PIE

HE WAS HANDSOME. He had a silken, sultry voice. His limber dance grooves single-handedly gave a generation of girls (and some boys) the vapors. But while I admire Elvis for all these wonders, nothing can compare to his introduction of bananas and peanut butter to the American food pantheon. Elvis may have left the building, but his pie lives on.

FOR THE CRUST		
Quick Puff Pastry (page 22)	⅛ batch	
FOR THE FILLING		
sweetened condensed milk	1 (14-ounce) can	1 (396-g) can
unsalted butter	½ cup	115 g
dark brown sugar, firmly packed	½ cup	110 g
creamy peanut butter	½ cup	120 ml
salt	½ teaspoon	3 g
vanilla bean paste	1 teaspoon	5 ml
ripe (but not overly ripe) bananas	4	
eggs	4	
FOR THE ASSEMBLY		
heavy cream	1 cup	240 ml
high-quality bittersweet or semisweet chocolate, at room temperature, for making chocolate curls	1 (7-ounce) bar	1 (200-gm) bar

Procedure for the crust

1. Preheat the oven to 350°F (175°C). Line a 9-inch (23-cm) pie plate with the dough, dock it, and freeze for 20 minutes.

2. Line the crust with parchment, fill it with pie weights or dried beans, and bake it for 20 minutes. Remove the parchment and pie weights and bake the crust for 15 to 20 minutes more, or until the bottom is golden brown and baked through. Set it aside to cool completely.

Procedure for the filling

1. Remove the label from the can of condensed milk. Poke 2 vent holes in the top of the can with a can opener and place it in a deep saucepan. Fill the saucepan with water until it reaches three-quarters of the way up the side of the can. Place the saucepan over medium heat, bring the water to a simmer, and let it cook for 2 hours, keeping an eye on the water level in the saucepan. Never let the water fall to less than halfway down the can. (We're technically making dulce de leche, if you must know.)

2. Let the can cool enough that you can handle it, open it completely, and scrape the contents into a clean saucepan. Add the butter, brown sugar, peanut butter, salt, and vanilla and stir over low heat until the butter has completely melted and the mixture comes to a boil. Stir constantly for a few minutes. The resulting toffee mixture should get a little more brown, but do not let it burn.

3. Preheat the oven to 325°F (165°C). Cut the bananas in ¼- to ½-inch (6- to 12-mm) slices and arrange them in an even layer on the bottom of the crust. It's okay to overlap the slices.

4. Whisk the eggs, then slowly pour the warm toffee mixture into them, whisking until the filling is smooth. Pour the toffee mixture on top of the sliced bananas and into the crust and bake for 45 minutes to 1 hour, just until the pie has set. Allow to cool completely.

Assembly

Whip the cream to stiff peaks and swirl it on top of the custard with the back of a spoon or a small offset spatula. Make sure your chocolate is at room temperature or slightly warmer (not to the point of melting; you just want it to grate easily and into lovely little swirls). Using a vegetable peeler, shave chocolate curls onto the top of the pie to taste. Refrigerate or serve immediately.

OPTION!

Fry 3 strips of bacon until very crispy. Crumble and sprinkle the bacon over pie just before serving.

Butterscotch MERINGUE PIE

MAKES 1
(9-INCH/23-CM) PIE

BUTTERSCOTCH DOES NOT CONTAIN SCOTCH. It never did. Let's just start there. The scotch in the butterscotch refers to how the candy was scored or "scotched" as it cooled, allowing the candy maker to easily break the hard, sweet stuff into even pieces.

The integral ingredient that it does contain is brown sugar, which, in its modern incarnation, is processed granulated sugar that's been infused with molasses. That is what gives homemade butterscotch its pleasing flavor, although I'd never stop you from drinking a glass of scotch while you conjure up this delicious pie.

FOR THE CRUST		
Simple Tart Dough (page 21)	½ batch	
FOR THE CARAMEL LINING		
granulated sugar	1 cup	200 g
heavy cream	½ cup	120 ml
unsalted butter	2 tablespoons	28 g
salt	½ teaspoon	3 g
FOR THE FILLING		
dark brown sugar, firmly packed	¾ cup	165 g
vanilla bean paste	2 tablespoons	30 ml
cornstarch	¼ cup	32 g
egg yolks	4	
salt	½ teaspoon	3 g
whole milk, divided	1½ cups	360 ml
heavy cream	1½ cups	360 ml
FOR THE ASSEMBLY		
dark brown sugar, firmly packed	1 cup	220 g
egg whites	4	
salt	pinch	

Procedure for the crust

1. Preheat the oven to 350°F (175°C). Roll the dough into a rough 11-inch (28-cm) round. Line a 9-inch (23-cm) pie plate with it and crimp the sides decoratively. Dock the bottom and freeze it for 20 minutes.

2. Line the crust with parchment, fill it with pie weights or dried beans, and bake it for 15 minutes. Remove the parchment and pie weights. Bake the crust for 20 minutes more, or until it is golden brown and baked through. Set it aside to cool completely.

Procedure for the caramel lining

Combine the granulated sugar, cream, butter, and salt in a heavy-bottomed saucepan over low heat and cook, stirring, until the sugar has melted. Clip on a candy thermometer and heat until the caramel reaches 240°F (116°C), then allow it to cool completely.

Procedure for the filling

1. Whisk together the brown sugar, vanilla, cornstarch, egg yolks, salt, and ½ cup (120 ml) of the milk in a mixing bowl.

2. Heat the remaining milk and the cream in a saucepan over medium heat until it comes to a simmer. Slowly pour the milk-cream mixture into the sugar mixture, whisking constantly until smooth.

3. Return the mixture to the saucepan and cook it over medium heat, whisking, until it thickens to the consistency of mayonnaise. Transfer the custard to a bowl, and cover the top with a piece of plastic wrap laid directly on the surface to prevent a skin from forming. Set aside to cool to room temperature.

Assembly

1. Pour the caramel into the cooled crust and smooth it along the bottom and sides, using a small offset spatula. Spoon the custard over the caramel and refrigerate the pie until the filling is cool and set.

2. Begin making a meringue by combining the brown sugar and ⅓ cup (75 ml) water in a heavy saucepan over low heat, stirring until the sugar has melted. Attach a candy thermometer and heat the sugar mixture until it reaches 234°F (112°C).

3. While the sugar syrup is cooking, place the egg whites and salt in the bowl of an electric mixer fitted with the whisk attachment. Whisk until the egg whites are foamy.

4. Once the sugar syrup has reached temperature, turn the mixer to medium-low and pour the sugar along the inside of the bowl (not directly into the egg whites, to keep from scrambling the eggs). Increase the mixer speed to high and whisk until you achieve stiff peaks.

5. Top the custard layer with the meringue, creating swirls and peaks with the back of a spoon. Gently brown the meringue with a kitchen torch. Do not use a broiler to brown the meringue, as this will melt the custard.

CHEWY
and
CHOCOLATY

TATE IS A YOUNG GIRL OF DISCERNING CULINARY TASTES. When I asked what kind of pie she'd like me to make her, she replied, "Chocolate." I assumed that, being a twelve-year-old girl, she'd lean toward the lighter side of chocolate, maybe even (shudder!) *milk*. (I don't know what I'd have done if she'd said *white*! Ye gads!).

But something told me I'd better ask her before jumping to conclusions. "What kind of chocolate?" Her answer pleased me immeasurably: "Dark. As dark as you can find." So it follows that this dark chocolate pie would have to be named after the chocolate connoisseur herself.

TATE
PIE

MAKES 1
(9-INCH/23-CM) PIE

FOR THE CRUST		
Simple Tart Dough (page 21)	½ batch	
FOR THE GANACHE		
heavy cream	¼ cup	60 ml
unsalted butter	2 tablespoons	28 g
vanilla extract	1 teaspoon	5 ml
bittersweet chocolate, chopped into small pieces	1 (3.5-ounce) bar	1 (100-g) bar
FOR THE MOUSSE		
unsalted butter	½ cup	115 g
instant espresso powder	1 tablespoon	3 g
eggs, separated	4	
heavy cream	½ cup	120 ml
half-and-half	½ cup	120 ml
vanilla extract	2 tablespoons	30 ml
sugar	½ cup	100 g
bittersweet (70%) chocolate, chopped into small pieces	10 ounces	280 g
lemon juice	1 squirt	
salt	pinch	
FOR THE ASSEMBLY		
heavy cream	1 cup	240 ml
bittersweet (70%) chocolate, chopped into small pieces	4 ounces	115 g

Procedure for the crust

1. Preheat the oven to 350°F (175°C). Line a 9-inch (23-cm) pie plate with the dough. Dock the bottom and freeze it for 20 minutes.

2. Line the crust with parchment, fill it with pie weights or dried beans, and bake it for 15 minutes. Remove the pie weights and parchment and

bake the crust for 10 minutes more, or until the bottom begins to turn golden brown and is cooked through. Set it aside to cool completely.

Procedure for the ganache

In a heavy saucepan over low heat, combine the cream, butter, and vanilla, stirring until the butter has completely melted. Increase the heat to medium-high and bring the mixture to a simmer. Remove the pot from the heat and pour in the chopped chocolate. Leave the pot undisturbed for a few minutes to allow the chocolate to melt. Whisk until the ganache has emulsified and is shiny.

Procedure for the mousse

1. Place a large metal bowl over a saucepan of boiling water. Combine the butter and espresso powder in the bowl as the butter melts.

2. In a mixing bowl, whisk together the egg yolks, cream, half-and-half, vanilla, and ¼ cup (50 g) of the sugar. Pour the mixture slowly into the butter in the metal bowl, whisking constantly, and continue to cook, whisking, over the simmering water until the mixture thickens.

3. Remove the metal bowl from the heat, add the chocolate pieces, and allow the mix to sit for at least 5 minutes. Whisk until the chocolate has completely melted and the mixture is smooth and completely combined. Set it aside.

4. In a small saucepan, combine the remaining sugar along with 2 tablespoons (30 ml) water and the lemon juice. Cook the mixture over low heat until the sugar completely melts. Increase the heat to medium-high, clip a candy thermometer to the pan, and heat it to 234°F (112°C).

5. Meanwhile, in the bowl of an electric mixer fitted with the whisk attachment, combine the egg whites and salt and whisk until foamy. When the sugar syrup reaches temperature, slowly pour it down the side of the mixing bowl. Mix until the egg whites hold a stiff peak, but do not overbeat so that they become dry. Add half of the egg-white mixture to the chocolate mixture and stir until no white streaks remain. Gently fold in the remaining egg whites.

Assembly

1. Pour the ganache into the crust and, using the back of a spoon or an offset spatula, spread it along the bottom and up the sides until the inside of the crust is completely coated. Refrigerate until the ganache has set, at least 15 minutes.

2. Once the ganache has set, pour half of the mousse into the crust. Refrigerate again while you make the whipped cream.

3. Thoroughly clean your mixer bowl and whisk attachment. Add the cream and beat until it holds stiff peaks. Fold the whipped cream into the remaining mousse and continue folding until no white streaks remain. Gently spoon the lightened mousse on top of the darker mousse and spread it carefully and evenly until it just touches the edges of the dough. Chill the pie in the freezer for at least 1 hour to set.

4. Before serving, melt the chocolate pieces and drizzle chocolate over the pie.

A NOTE FROM THE SWEETIE PIE

If I've said it once, I've said it a million times: The quality of the chocolate you use in pastry work is paramount to success. It's heartening that many grocery stores now carry great brands like Guittard, Lindt, and Scharffen Berger in the bakery aisle. But *my* all-time favorites for chocolate to work with (and to eat straight up) are Callebaut's 60/40 and Valrhona's Le Noir. The 60/40 refers to the percentage of cocoa; the "Le Noir" falls just a little below 60 percent. And while you might think, "I'll just look for any old chocolate that says it's within the 60 percent range," I'd caution you. The two I've mentioned have a lovely balance between glorious chocolate flavor and just enough sweetness. I find that most other brands might boast a high percentage of cocoa but are so cloyingly sweet that the taste of cocoa is lost.

The percentage also makes a difference in the workings of the recipes. With a lower or higher percentage, other ratios within a chocolate recipe have to be changed. Say you want to use milk chocolate in a mousse instead—it won't set the way a dark-chocolate mousse would, and you'll likely have to add gelatin to achieve the desired firmness. The cocoa acts as a firming agent, and you need a specific ratio to make the recipe work properly.

As for cocoa powder, I use Callebaut's Extra Brute and Valrhona's Cocoa Gastronomie exclusively. Period. No substitutions in my kitchen. They are simply the best, in my opinion. If you don't have a restaurant-supply shop that sells these brands near you (I've found them at Whole Foods and higher-end grocery stores), they're readily available online.

THIS IS A SOPHISTICATED CANDY BAR WRAPPED UP IN TART'S CLOTHING. It features caramel that leaves ropy tendrils behind after you've taken a bite. And while you can use a fork, I have to tell you it's so much easier to pick up your slice to convey it to your mandibles.

FOR THE CRUST		
Chocolate Cookie Tart Crust (page 31)	½ batch	
Soft Caramel Filling (page 36)	1 batch	
FOR THE TRUFFLES		
heavy cream	¾ cup	177 ml
unsalted butter	2 tablespoons	28 g
salt	pinch	
corn syrup (optional)	1 tablespoon	15 ml
bittersweet chocolate, finely chopped	8 ounces	225 g
cocoa powder	¼ cup	20 g
FOR THE ASSEMBLY		
large-grain fleur de sel (sea salt)	½ teaspoon	2.5 g

MAKES 1
(8-INCH/20-CM) TART

Procedure for the crust

1. Preheat the oven to 350°F (175°C). Line an 8-inch (20-cm) tart pan with the dough. Dock and freeze it for 20 minutes. Line the crust with parchment, fill it with pie weights, and bake it for 15 minutes. Remove the pie weights and parchment and bake the crust for 15 minutes more, or until the bottom is golden brown and baked through. Allow it to cool.

2. Prepare the caramel filling as instructed on page 36 and pour it into the cooled crust. Refrigerate until firm, about 2 hours.

Procedure for the truffles

1. In a small, heavy saucepan, simmer together the cream, butter, salt, and corn syrup, if using, making sure the butter melts completely. Take the pan from the heat and add the chocolate. Allow it to sit for a few minutes undisturbed, then whisk the mixture until the glaze emulsifies and all the chocolate melts. Cover and refrigerate until set, about 1 hour.

2. Using a melon scoop, a teaspoon-sized cookie scoop, or a teaspoon, form small rounds of ganache and roll them into balls with your hands. Roll the truffles in cocoa powder to coat them evenly.

Assembly

1. Place the truffles around the perimeter of the tart, sprinkle fleur de sel over all, and serve at room temperature.

Chocolate STOUT Pudding PIE

MAKES 1
(8-INCH/20-CM) TART

WE VERMONTERS ARE KNOWN PRIMARILY FOR OUR MAPLE SYRUP AND OUR CHEESE, BUT DID YOU KNOW WE ALSO HAVE A BEVY OF LOCAL BREWERIES THAT DO MAGIC WITH HOPS AND BARLEY? Well, we do. I'm as adventurous as the next gal when it comes to trying new and exciting variations on the beer theme, and I had a few bottles of Harpoon chocolate stout in the fridge that I just couldn't bring myself to drink. Of course, I had plenty of ideas for how to use it for dessert!

Once St. Patrick's Day rolled around, I found myself compelled to grab a bottle opener and see what I could whip up with a bit of kitchen alchemy. This dark beauty is the result.

FOR THE CRUST		
Sweet Tart Dough (page 30)	½ batch	
FOR THE FILLING		
cocoa powder (I use Callebaut Extra Brute)	½ cup	40 g
maple syrup	½ cup	120 ml
chocolate stout	1 (12-ounce) bottle	1 (360-ml) bottle
cornstarch	¼ cup	32 g
egg yolks	4	
salt	pinch	
vanilla extract	1 teaspoon	5 ml
heavy cream	1½ cups	360 ml
FOR THE ASSEMBLY		
heavy cream	1 cup	240 ml
confectioners' sugar	¼ cup	25 g
bittersweet chocolate, at room temperature, for making chocolate curls	1 bar or large piece	

Procedure for the crust

1. Preheat the oven to 350°F (175°C). Line an 8-inch (20-cm) tart pan with the dough. Dock and freeze it for 20 minutes.

2. Line the crust with parchment, fill it with pie weights or dried beans, and bake it for 15 minutes. Remove the pie weights and parchment and bake the crust for 15 minutes more, or until the bottom is golden brown and baked through.

Procedure for the filling

1. Whisk together the cocoa powder, maple syrup, chocolate stout, cornstarch, egg yolks, salt, and vanilla in the bowl of a stand mixer fitted with the whisk attachment.

2. In a large saucepan, bring the cream to a simmer.

3. With the mixer running on low, carefully pour the hot cream into the cocoa mixture. Whisk until completely combined.

4. Transfer the liquid back into the saucepan and cook it over medium heat, whisking, until it thickens to a pudding.

5. Immediately pour the pudding into the prepared crust. Cover the pie with a sheet of plastic wrap, making sure the plastic is laid directly on the surface of the pudding to prevent a skin from forming. Refrigerate the pie until it's set, at least 2 hours.

Assembly

1. Clean the mixer bowl and whisk attachment and whisk the cream and confectioners' sugar until you achieve stiff peaks.

2. Fill a pastry bag fitted with a large open tip with the whipped cream and decorate the top of the pie. Using a very sharp vegetable peeler, shave curls from the chocolate and sprinkle them over all.

CHOCOLATE CREAM *Pie*

MAKES 1
(9-INCH/23-CM) PIE

I DID NOT KNOW THE JOY THAT COULD BE FOUND IN A SINGLE SLICE OF PIE. I did not know it until I made it, combining extra pastry cream with some ganache. One taste and I knew this glorious succulence deserved a buttery and flaky vessel to contain it. And I made it so, but first I lined the bottom of my crust with a dark coating of pure ganache, a kind of fitted sheet atop the crunchy mattress that was my quick puff. And then I ladled in the filling. Feeling unstoppable, I layered on lush whipped cream, a top sheet of fluffy glory. I shaved a bit of chocolate over the whole yummy mess. The first slice was mine, and I never looked back.

FOR THE CRUST		
Quick Puff Pastry (page 22)	⅛ batch	
FOR THE GANACHE		
bittersweet chocolate, finely chopped	8 ounces	225 g
heavy cream	¾ cup	177 ml
unsalted butter	2 tablespoons	28 g
corn syrup	1 tablespoon	15 ml
salt	pinch	
FOR THE ASSEMBLY		
Pastry Cream (page 35)	½ batch	
heavy cream	1 cup	240 ml
high-quality bittersweet or semisweet chocolate, at room temperature, for making curls	1 bar or large piece	

Procedure for the crust

1. Preheat the oven to 350°F (175°C). Roll out the dough and use it to line a 9-inch (23-cm) pie plate. Dock and freeze it for 20 minutes.

2. Line the crust with parchment, fill it with pie weights or dried beans, and bake it for 20 minutes. Remove the pie weights and parchment and bake the crust for 10 to 15 minutes more, or until the bottom is golden brown and cooked through. Set it aside to cool completely, about 1 hour.

Procedure for the ganache

Place the chocolate in a mixing bowl and set it aside. Combine the cream, butter, and corn syrup in a saucepan over medium-high heat and bring the mixture to a simmer. Pour the cream mixture over the chocolate and allow everything to sit for at least 1 minute. Whisk until the mixture is smooth. Cover the ganache with plastic wrap and allow it to come to room temperature, but don't allow it to set completely—it should have a peanut butter–like spreadability by this stage.

Assembly

1. Spoon about ¼ cup (60 ml) of the ganache into the crust and spread it evenly along the bottom and sides. (If the ganache isn't easily spreadable, gently heat it over simmering water until it just loosens.) Chill until set, about 15 minutes.

2. Stir 1 cup (240 ml) of the ganache into the pastry cream until the mixture is smooth. Pour this into the ganache-lined crust and spread it into an even layer. Chill the pie until it is set, at least 2 hours.

3. Once the ganache filling has set, pour the cream into a bowl and whisk until it is stiff. Smooth the cream over the chocolate filling with the back of a spoon or an offset spatula. Using a very sharp vegetable peeler, shave curls from the chocolate onto the top of the pie.

A NOTE FROM THE SWEETIE PIE

Oftentimes, when making a batch of ganache for a recipe you will have a nice amount left over, so I suggest you make truffles. Allow the ganache to set completely and then, using a melon scoop, a teaspoon-sized cookie scoop, or a teaspoon, form small balls of chocolate. Roll them in your hands to make them uniform and then dust them with cocoa. (Wearing latex gloves makes this a much cleaner task!) Serve them with the cream pie for an added dose of bittersweet.

Chocolate ORANGE SOUFFLÉ Tartlets

MAKES 10
(4-INCH/10-CM) TARTLETS

WHEN I WAS A KID, THERE WAS A PARTICULAR CANDY I BECAME ADDICTED TO IN GERMANY (SHOCKING, ISN'T IT?). I know, I know—I'm addicted to candy in general, but this was an odd sort of confection to find irresistible. The little nuggets are called *Erfrischungsstäbchen*, which translates to "refreshment sticks."

They are little bites of citrus liquid wrapped in a candy shell that's surrounded by dark chocolate. The chocolate is as smooth and bitter as you'd want it to be. The thin sugar candy coating brings a slight crunch to the proceedings, and there's just enough liquid filling that the lemon or orange (the box contains both!) gently coats your tongue. They all mix together in a glorious symphony of, well, quite frankly, refreshment. This tart is as close to my childhood obsession as I can get without boarding a Lufthansa flight to Munich, and I've added the mature element of soufflé. The flavor combination may be timeless, but a girl's palate does evolve, after all.

Chocolate Cookie Tart Dough (page 31)	1 batch	
unsalted butter	¾ cup	170 g
bittersweet chocolate, finely chopped	8 ounces	225 g
orange extract	2 teaspoons	10 ml
zest of 1 orange, plus additional long curls of zest for decoration		
eggs	5	
sugar	1 cup, plus 2 tablespoons	200 g, plus 25 g
salt	½ teaspoon	3 g
all-purpose flour	¼ cup	30 g

1. Preheat the oven to 325°F (165°C). Line 10 (4-inch/10-cm) flan tart rings with the dough. Dock the dough and freeze it for 20 minutes. Line the crusts with parchment, fill them with pie weights or dried beans, and bake them for 15 minutes. Remove the pie weights and parchment and bake the crusts for 10 minutes more, or until they are baked through.

2. In a large metal bowl over a simmering pot of water, melt the butter and chopped chocolate. Stir in the orange extract and grated zest and keep the mixture warm.

3. In the bowl of an electric mixer fitted with the whisk attachment, whisk together the eggs, 1 cup (200 g) of the sugar, and the salt on high speed until the mixture turns light yellow and thickens to the point that it ribbons when the whisk is lifted from the eggs. Sift the flour over the egg mixture and gently fold it in.

4. Take one-third of the egg mixture and vigorously mix it into the chocolate mixture to lighten the batter. Gently fold the remaining egg mixture into the chocolate.

5. Divide the chocolate filling among the cooled crusts, sprinkle the remaining sugar evenly over the tops, and freeze the tartlets for at least 2 hours.

6. Preheat the oven to 325°F (165°C). Bake the tartlets for 15 minutes, or just until the filling puffs (it will crack a little—this is good). Top each tartlet with a ribbon of orange zest and serve warm.

Fleur de Sel Caramel Almond
BROWNIE
PIE

MAKES 1
(9-INCH/23-CM) SQUARE PIE

CRUNCHY, CHEWY—SALTY!—CRUNCHY, CHEWY. This pie is a splendiferous compendium of the most compelling elements of dessert, with solid doses of chocolate, caramel, and nuttiness. And those particular ingredients alternate, one on top of the other, to supply a textural party as well as a taste sensation in every bite. Add a scoop of creamy vanilla ice cream, and you're set for life.

FOR THE CRUST		
unsalted butter	½ cup	115 g
sugar	1 cup	200 g
salt	1 teaspoon	6 g
eggs	2	
vanilla bean paste	1 tablespoon	15 ml
all-purpose flour	½ cup	60 g
dark cocoa powder	1 cup	85 g
FOR THE FILLING		
sugar	1 cup	200 g
salt	1 teaspoon	6 g
lemon juice	1 squirt	
heavy cream	½ cup	120 ml
unsalted butter	2 tablespoons	28 g
Pastry Cream (page 35), prepared through step 2	1 batch	
FOR THE ASSEMBLY		
½ cup dry-roasted, salted almonds		
heavy cream	1½ cups	360 ml

Procedure for the crust

1. In the bowl of a stand mixer fitted with the paddle attachment, mix the butter, sugar, and salt until just combined. Add the eggs one at a time, and then the vanilla.

2. In a small bowl, whisk together the flour and cocoa powder. With the mixer on low speed, slowly add the cocoa mixture to the egg mixture and stir until just combined. Cover the bowl with plastic wrap and refrigerate it for 30 minutes.

3. Preheat the oven to 350°F (175°C). Prepare a 9-inch (23-cm) square tart pan with nonstick spray with flour. (This is important. If you don't have nonstick spray with flour, spray the pan first and then dust it with flour.

Otherwise, your crust will stick horribly.) Spoon the batter into the prepared pan and smooth it out with a small offset spatula.

4. Bake the crust for 20 minutes. Remove the crust from the oven and cover the top with parchment paper (this is going to feel backwards, but trust me), then a layer of pie weights, and press down gently. Add more weights—as many as will fit on top of the parchment without rolling off—and bake for 10 minutes more.

5. Remove the crust from the oven, but leave the weights on top until it has completely cooled.

Procedure for the filling

1. Place the sugar, salt, lemon juice, and ⅓ cup (75 ml) water in a saucepan and cook the mixture, stirring, over low heat until the sugar crystals melt completely. With a wet pastry brush, brush down the sides of the pot to remove any sugar crystals that might be clinging there.

2. Turn the heat to high and cook the sugar syrup until it turns a light amber. Take the pot from the heat and carefully add the cream and butter. Stand back—the caramel will bubble vigorously. Stir until everything is completely incorporated. Set the pan aside.

3. Prepare the pastry cream recipe on page 35 through step 2. Then, with the mixer running on low to prevent splashing, carefully pour the hot cream mixture into the egg-yolk mixture. Scrape down the sides and the bottom of the bowl to loosen any stubborn cornstarch. Mix for a few more seconds. Transfer the mixture back to the saucepan. Add ½ cup (120 ml) of the caramel you just made, reserving the rest for assembling the pie (in other words, don't eat it).

4. Whisk the caramel pastry cream over medium heat until it thickens to the consistency of mayonnaise. This can take a few minutes, but be patient.

5. Pour the pastry cream through a fine sieve and into a bowl. Cover the top of with a piece of plastic wrap laid directly on the surface to prevent a skin from forming, and refrigerate it until set, about 2 hours.

Assembly

1. Remove the weights and parchment from the crust, and spread ½ cup (120 ml) of the reserved caramel from edge to edge. If the caramel has hardened, gently heat it over low heat until it is loose enough to spread.

2. Layer the almonds evenly on top of the caramel. Refrigerate the pie until the caramel has set, at least 30 minutes.

3. Gently stir the pastry cream with a wooden spoon to loosen and smooth it. (As pastry cream cools, it becomes very firm—this is normal, so don't worry.) Put ½ cup (120 ml) of the pastry cream in the bowl of an electric mixer and set it aside.

4. Transfer the remaining pastry cream to a pastry bag fitted with a large open tip. Pipe the cream in an even layer onto the pie, on top of the almonds. Use a small offset spatula to smooth out the cream in an even layer. Return the pie to the fridge while you make the whipped cream.

5. Add the cream to the mixing bowl with the reserved caramel pastry cream. Using a stand mixer fitted with the whisk attachment, whisk the pastry cream on high until it holds stiff peaks. Transfer it to a pastry bag fitted with a large star tip. Decoratively pipe the whipped cream onto the entire surface of the pie. If you have any caramel remaining, drizzle it on top of the pie just before serving.

FOR YEARS, I RAILED AGAINST THE HORROR THAT WAS COCO-NUT. I could not, I would not, allow a shred of the tropical stuff to touch my lips. I can be such an idiot. As it turns out, I like coconut very much. Whatever the 1970s incarnation was that had me cringing since childhood must have been a culinary doozy, because there's very little made with coconut that I won't eat now.

This particular nest of chewy, crunchy, coconutty happiness is my particular favorite.

Coconut Birds'
NESTS

MAKES ABOUT 15
LITTLE NESTS

FOR THE COCONUT NESTS		
egg whites	4	
sweetened shredded coconut	3½ cups	315 g
sugar	¾ cup	150 g
vanilla extract	1 teaspoon	5 ml
salt	½ teaspoon	3 g
FOR THE CARAMEL		
sugar	1 cup	200 g
lemon juice	1 squirt	
salt	1 teaspoon	6 g
heavy cream	½ cup	120 ml
unsalted butter	2 tablespoons	28 g
FOR THE GANACHE		
heavy cream	½ cup	120 ml
unsalted butter	2 tablespoons	28 g
corn syrup	1 tablespoon	15 ml
bittersweet chocolate, chopped	8 ounces	225 g
salt	pinch	

Procedure for the coconut nests

1. Preheat the oven to 300°F (150°C). Combine the egg whites, coconut, sugar, vanilla, and salt in a metal bowl. Set the bowl over a saucepan of simmering water and cook, stirring occasionally to prevent the bottom from burning. Cook until the mixture is hot and has thickened slightly, about 10 minutes.

2. With a medium-sized cookie scoop, drop the batter onto a parchment-lined sheet pan in baseball-sized mounds. Gently press down in the middle of each one to form a bird's-nest shape. Bake the nests for 15 to 20 minutes, or until the edges are dark golden brown. Allow them to cool completely.

Procedure for the caramel

1. In a large, heavy saucepan, combine the sugar, ⅓ cup (75 ml) water, the lemon juice, and salt. Stir over medium-low heat until the sugar has completely melted. Take a damp pastry brush and wipe the sides of the saucepan to wash away any errant sugar crystals. Stop stirring, turn the heat up to medium-high, and clip on a sugar thermometer. Heat the syrup to 245°F (120°C).

2. Take the pan from the stove and carefully add the cream and butter—the mixture will bubble vigorously. Stir until the butter and cream are fully integrated. Allow the caramel to cool for about 1 hour.

Procedure for the ganache

In a small, heavy saucepan, heat the cream and butter to a simmer, then remove the pan from the stovetop and add the chocolate. Allow it to sit undisturbed for 5 minutes. Whisk until the chocolate is completely melted and the ganache is smooth. Allow it to cool until it has thickened enough to keep its shape when piped, about 1 hour.

Assembly

Divide the caramel among the nests. Transfer the ganache to a large pastry bag fitted with a large star tip and pipe rosettes on top of the caramel. Serve the nests immediately, at room temperature.

TART
and
TROPICAL

LEMON
Tartlets

MAKES 8
(4-INCH/10-CM) TARTLETS

FOR A PLATE OF SUNSHINE, LOOK NO FURTHER THAN THIS TANGY AND BUTTERY SLIP OF A TART. The smooth tartness of the lemon contrasts beautifully with the crunchy sweet of the crust and the fluffy delicacy of the meringue. Be sure to use freshly squeezed lemon juice for the best flavor.

FOR THE CRUSTS		
Sweet Tart Dough (page 30), Lemon citrus option	½ batch	
FOR THE FILLING		
unflavored gelatin	1 teaspoon	2.5 g
lemon juice, divided	2 tablespoons, plus 1 cup	30 ml, plus 240 ml
sugar	2 cups	400 g
egg yolks	14	
unsalted butter	2 tablespoons	28 g
FOR THE ASSEMBLY		
egg whites	about 5 (5/8 cup)	150 ml
salt	pinch	
sugar	1 cup	200 g
lemon juice	1 teaspoon	5 ml

Procedure for the crusts

1. Preheat the oven to 325°F (165°C). Divide the dough into 8 even pieces and use them to line 8 (4-inch/10-cm) flan rings. Dock the bottom of the dough and freeze the tarts for 20 minutes.

2. Line each crust with parchment and fill it with pie weights or dried beans. Bake the crusts for 15 minutes. Remove the weights and parchment and bake them for 15 minutes more, or until the bottoms are golden brown and baked through. Set the crusts aside and allow them to cool completely.

Procedure for the filling

1. Meanwhile, in a small bowl, sprinkle the gelatin on top of 2 tablespoons (30 ml) of the lemon juice until it's "bloomed" and looks soggy. Set it aside.

2. In a heatproof metal bowl, combine the remaining 1 cup (240 ml) lemon juice, the sugar, and the egg yolks. Place the bowl over a pot of simmering water and whisk until the mixture has thickened enough that

Passion Fruit Chiffon Tartlets

Lemon Tartlets

it ribbons when you pull out the whisk. Take the bowl off the heat and immediately add the gelatin mixture, whisking until it's completely melted. Add the butter and whisk until it's fully incorporated.

3. Immediately divide the curd among the crusts and refrigerate the tartlets until the filling sets, about 2 hours.

Assembly

1. In the bowl of an electric mixer fitted with the whisk attachment, combine the egg whites and salt and whisk until light and foamy.

2. In the meantime, add the sugar, ½ cup (120 ml) water, and the lemon juice to a heavy saucepan. Cook, stirring, over low heat until the sugar is completely melted. Clip on a candy thermometer and heat the syrup to 234°F (112°C).

3. With the mixer running on medium-high speed, carefully pour the sugar syrup down the side of the bowl into the egg whites. Increase the speed to high and whip until you achieve very stiff white peaks.

4. Transfer the meringue to a pastry bag fitted with a star tip and pipe it onto the lemon tartlets in a decorative pattern.

5. Brown the meringue with a kitchen torch. (Do not place under a broiler, as that would melt the curd.)

CHIFFON IS WHAT HAPPENS WHEN YOU ADD THE EGG WHITES BACK INTO A CURD. It lightens the pie and makes it reach for the *sky*! Passion fruit is a beautiful and complex fruit—it brings elegance to what is usually a very homespun dessert. If you cannot find passion-fruit puree, substitute the same amount of passion-fruit juice (Goya brand is readily available) and decrease the sugar in the curd mixture to ½ cup (100 g).

Passion Fruit
CHIFFON
TARTLETS

MAKES 8
(4-INCH/10-CM) TARTLETS

FOR THE CRUSTS		
Sweet Tart Dough (page 30), Lemon citrus option	½ batch	
FOR THE FILLING		
unflavored gelatin	1 teaspoon	2.5 g
passion fruit puree, divided	2 tablespoons, plus 1 cup	30 ml, plus 240 ml
sugar, divided	2 cups	400 g
eggs, separated	14	
unsalted butter	2 tablespoons	28 g
salt	pinch	
lemon juice	1 squirt	

Procedure for the crusts

1. Preheat the oven to 325°F (165°C). Divide the dough into 8 even pieces and use them to line 8 (4-inch/10-cm) flan rings. Dock the bottom of the dough and freeze the tarts for 20 minutes.

2. Line each crust with parchment and fill it with pie weights or dried beans. Bake the crusts for 15 minutes. Remove the weights and parchment and bake them for 15 minutes more, or until the bottoms are golden brown and baked through. Set the crusts aside and allow them to cool completely.

Procedure for the filling

1. In a small bowl, sprinkle the gelatin on top of 2 tablespoons (30 ml) of the puree until it's "bloomed" and looks soggy. Set it aside.

2. In a heatproof metal bowl, combine the remaining 1 cup (240 ml) puree, 1 cup (200 g) of the sugar, and the egg yolks. Place the bowl over a pot of simmering water and whisk until the lemon mixture has thickened enough that it ribbons when you pull out the whisk. Take the pan off the heat and immediately add the gelatin mixture; whisk until it's completely melted. Add the butter and whisk until it's fully incorporated.

3. In the *clean* bowl of a stand mixer fitted with the whisk attachment, whisk the egg whites with the salt until the mixture is light and foamy.

4. In the meantime, combine the remaining 1 cup (200g) sugar with the lemon juice and ⅓ cup (75 ml) water in a heavy saucepan over low heat, stirring until the sugar melts. Attach a candy thermometer and heat the syrup until the temperature reaches 234°F (112°C). With the mixer on low speed, slowly pour the hot syrup into the egg whites, increasing the speed to high once all the syrup is added. Whisk until you achieve stiff white peaks, making sure not to overbeat, as this will make the meringue dry and chunky.

5. Gently fold the meringue into the passion-fruit curd until no white streaks remain. Divide the passion-fruit chiffon equally among the crusts. Using a small offset spatula, create an attractive and cloudlike mound of fluffy goodness. Chill.

A CRISPY, BUTTERY, SWEET SHELL FILLED WITH A TANGY, SWEET, CREAMY PUDDING AND A SPONGY CAKE. How is this possible, when only one batter is poured into the tart shell?

It's magic, of course. Baking magic. In the heat of the oven, the batter separates into two distinct and delicious entities. The bottom layer is really a pudding. The top layer is really a spongy cake. Don't ask me to explain how it's possible. I just make it (and eat it).

MEYER LEMON
Pudding Pie

MAKES 1
(8-INCH/20-CM) DEEP-DISH
PUDDING PIE

Sweet Tart Dough (page 30), Citrus option made with Meyer lemon zest	½ batch	
sugar	1 cup	200 g
unsalted butter, at room temperature	4 tablespoons	55 g
salt	1 teaspoon	6 g
eggs, separated	4	
Meyer lemon juice	½ cup	120 ml
Meyer lemon zest	1 tablespoon	6 g
buttermilk	1½ cups	360 ml
all-purpose flour	½ cup	60 g

1. Preheat the oven to 350°F (175°C). Place an 8-inch (20-cm) cake ring or springform pan on a baking sheet lined with parchment and coat the ring or pan with nonstick spray. Line the ring or pan with an even layer of dough, starting at the bottom and then building up the sides. Freeze the dough for 20 minutes.

2. Line the inside with parchment (use enough to give you handles to hold on to when you pull the weights out later) and fill the crust with pie weights or dried beans to the very rim of the ring or pan. Bake the crust for 20 minutes, then remove the weights and parchment, and bake it for 15 minutes more, or until the bottom portion of the dough no longer looks wet. Leave the oven on.

3. In the bowl of a stand mixer fitted with the paddle attachment, cream together the sugar, butter, and salt until light and fluffy. Add the egg yolks, one at a time, until each is completely incorporated, and then add the lemon juice, lemon zest, and buttermilk. Mix until the batter is smooth, making sure to scrape the bowl to loosen up any chunks of butter that continue to cling to the sides and bottom. Sift the flour over the top of the batter and fold it into the mixture with a large rubber spatula until it is fully incorporated. Transfer the batter to a large bowl.

4. Clean the mixing bowl and fit the mixer with the whisk attachment. (Make sure that the bowl is really clean, without a single trace of butter or any other kind of fat, as that will deflate your egg whites.) Beat the egg whites until they reach medium-stiff peaks, making sure not to overbeat to the point that the meringue dries out.

5. Gently fold the egg whites into the batter and pour the mixture into the prepared crust. Bake for 50 minutes to 1 hour, until the top has puffed and browned and the middle of the cake is no longer fluid. When you tap the pan, there will be a gentle wobble (not a liquid jiggle) in the middle of the cake (like a cheesecake); this will firm up once out of the oven.

6. Allow the cake to cool completely. Transfer it to a serving platter and gently run a knife along the sides of the cake ring or springform pan to release the cake.

THIS LOVELY TART PACKS A TROPICAL VACATION INTO EVERY SLIGHTLY CHEWY, SUBTLY CRUNCHY BITE. There's no need to shell out all that dough on a plane ticket and hotel room—really. Just bake this, take a bite, and shut your eyes.

Pineapple
COCONUT
Macaroon
TART

MAKES 1
(8-INCH/20-CM) ROUND
OR SQUARE TART

FOR THE CRUST		
Sweet Tart Dough (page 30), Macadamia nut option	½ batch	
FOR THE FILLING		
unsalted butter	½ cup	115 g
coconut milk	¼ cup	60 ml
eggs	3	
vanilla bean paste	1 teaspoon	5 ml
sweetened flaked coconut	1½ cups	128 g
sugar	1 cup	200 g
salt	½ teaspoon	3 g
lemon juice	1 tablespoon	15 ml
FOR THE ASSEMBLY		
pineapple rings (canned or fresh), cut in half	10	

Procedure for the crust

Preheat the oven to 350°F (175°C). Line an 8-inch (20-cm) fluted, round or square tart pan with the dough, then dock the bottom of the dough and freeze it for 20 minutes. Line the crust with parchment, fill it with pie weights or dried beans, and bake it for 20 minutes. Remove the pie weights and parchment and set the crust aside.

Procedure for the filling

1. In a small saucepan over medium heat, combine the butter and coconut milk; heat until the butter melts completely.

2. In a mixing bowl, whisk together the eggs and vanilla. Stir the coconut, sugar, and salt into the egg mixture, then gently stir in the coconut-milk mixture and the lemon juice until well combined.

Assembly

1. Arrange the pineapple pieces on the bottom of the crust, then scrape the macaroon filling on top of the pineapple slices and smooth it into an even layer with an offset spatula.

2. Bake the tart for 45 minutes to 1 hour, until the filling has puffed and set and is golden brown. Allow to cool completely before serving.

I DIDN'T KNOW I HAD A FIELD OF MINT IN MY BACKYARD UNTIL I LOST CONTROL OF MY RIDING MOWER AND SPED ACROSS THE HERBACEOUS PLOT LIKE A JOHN DEERE BAT FROM HELL. The refreshing perfume distracted me from my impending doom; I started concocting recipes as I rode to my demise. And then I remembered I only had to take my foot off the gas, and all was well. I had a plan, and a near-death experience wasn't going to keep me from it.

Ruby Red
MINTED TART

MAKES 1
(9-INCH/23-CM) TART

Sweet Tart Dough (page 30), Semolina option	½ batch	
Ruby Red grapefruits	2 to 3	
mint leaves	¼ cup, plus more for decoration	10 g, plus more for decoration
sweetened condensed milk	1 (14-ounce) can	1 (396-g) can
egg yolks	4	
salt	pinch	

1. Preheat the oven to 350°F (175°C). Line a 9-inch (23-cm) tart pan with the dough, then dock the bottom of the dough and freeze it for 20 minutes. Line the crust with parchment and fill it with pie weights or dried beans. Bake the crust for 20 minutes, remove the pie weights and parchment, and continue baking for 15 minutes more, or until the dough no longer looks wet.

2. Meanwhile, remove the zest from 1 grapefruit in a long ribbon and set it aside for decoration. Grate 1 tablespoon (6 g) zest from another grapefruit and set that aside. Squeeze the grapefruits so that you have ½ cup (120 ml) juice.

3. Muddle together the ¼ cup (10 g) mint leaves and the grapefruit juice. To do this, smoosh them together in a large bowl using a pestle or, if you don't have one, a wooden spoon. This will infuse the juice with the minty flavor. Pour the juice through a fine-mesh sieve into a mixing bowl; discard the mint.

4. Whisk together the strained grapefruit juice, zest, condensed milk, egg yolks, and salt. Pour the mixture into the prepared crust and bake the tart for 20 to 25 minutes, or until the filling is set.

5. Allow the tart to cool completely before serving. Top each slice with a whole mint leaf and arrange a grapefruit-peel curl on top of the mint.

Yuzu-Ginger Rice Pudding MERINGUE PIE

MAKES 1
(8-INCH/20-CM) PIE

YUZU IS AN ASIAN CITRUS FRUIT THAT RARELY MAKES AN APPEARANCE IN DESSERTS. It looks like a small grapefruit and tastes like a sour mandarin orange. Paired with a creamy rice pudding made of elegant jasmine rice, this lovely tart ends a meal with glorious brightness and a hint of sunshine. Look for yuzu juice online or in local Asian markets.

FOR THE RICE PUDDING		
whole milk	1 cup	240 ml
buttermilk	1 cup	240 ml
heavy cream	½ cup	120 ml
yuzu juice	½ cup	120 ml
long-grain jasmine rice	½ cup	92 g
sugar	¼ cup	50 g
salt	½ teaspoon	3 g
chopped crystallized ginger (I chop the pieces just slightly smaller than a kernel of corn)	¼ cup	35 g
FOR THE CRUST		
Simple Tart Dough (page 21)	½ batch	
FOR THE MERINGUE		
egg whites	5	
salt	pinch	
ground ginger	¼ teaspoon	1 g
sugar	1 cup	200 g
water	⅓ cup	75 ml
FOR THE ASSEMBLY		
large whole pieces of crystallized ginger cut into heart shapes		

Procedure for the rice pudding

1. In a heavy saucepan, combine the milk, buttermilk, cream, yuzu juice, and rice. Bring to a low boil and then reduce the heat and simmer until the rice is just tender, about 25 minutes. Stir constantly while cooking, as the rice tends to stick to the bottom of the pan.

2. Add the sugar and salt and continue to stir until the pudding has thickened, 5 to 10 minutes. Stir in the chopped ginger.

3. Transfer the rice pudding into a large bowl and cover the top with plastic wrap laid directly on the surface to prevent a skin from forming. Set the pudding aside to cool to room temperature.

Procedure for the crust

1. Preheat the oven to 350°F (175°C). Roll the dough into a loose 10-inch (25-cm) round between ⅛ and ¼ inch (3 and 6 mm) thick, then line an 8-inch (20-cm) tart pan with it. Trim the edges so they are flush with the rim of the pan, dock the dough, and freeze it for 20 minutes.

2. Line the crust with parchment, fill it with pie weights or dried beans, and bake it for 15 minutes. Remove the weights and parchment and bake the crust for 10 minutes more, or until the bottom is browned and baked through. Allow the crust to cool to room temperature.

Procedure for the meringue

1. Place the egg whites, salt, and ground ginger in the bowl of a stand mixer fitted with the whisk attachment. Whip until the egg whites become white and foamy (but don't mix to the point of stiff peaks or dryness).

2. Meanwhile, combine the sugar and water in a heavy saucepan over low heat, and cook, stirring, until the sugar granules have melted. Raise the heat to medium-high, stop stirring, attach a candy thermometer, and heat the syrup until the temperature reaches 234°F (112°C).

3. With the mixer running on medium-high speed, slowly pour the sugar syrup down the side of the mixing bowl and into the egg whites. Increase the speed to high and whip until you achieve stiff, white peaks.

Assembly

Spoon the rice pudding into the crust and smooth the surface with the back of a spoon. Transfer the meringue to a piping bag fitted with a star tip and pipe decorative dollops over the entire surface of the tart. Gently brown the meringue with a kitchen torch or under a broiler. Top with the ginger hearts. Serve immediately.

KEY LIME IS SUCH A HAPPY CITRUS—WHAT OTHER SOUR FRUIT BRINGS TO MIND TWO OF THE LOVELIEST THINGS ON THE PLANET, THE BEACH AND PIE, WHEN YOU UTTER HER NAME? And she never fails to please, this lovely pie. Key lime pie is as silky sweet and tangy as a lazy day on the soft sands of Florida. Mascarpone is a natural addition, providing an extra dose of creaminess and tang.

KEY LIME *Mascarpone Cream* **PIE**

MAKES 1
(8-INCH/20-CM) PIE

Sweet Tart Dough (page 30)	½ batch	
Key lime juice (I use Manhattan brand), divided	½ cup plus 3 tablespoons	120 ml, plus 45 ml
sweetened condensed milk	1 (14-ounce) can	1 (396-g) can
egg yolks	4	
salt	pinch	
mascarpone cheese	¼ cup	60 g
heavy cream	1 cup	240 ml
confectioners' sugar	¼ cup	25 g

1. Preheat the oven to 350°F (175°C). Line an 8-inch (20-cm) tart pan with the dough, then dock the bottom and freeze it for 20 minutes. Line the crust with parchment, fill it with pie weights or dried beans, and bake it for 20 minutes. Remove the weights and lining, then bake the crust for 15 minutes more, or until it no longer has a raw-dough sheen.

2. For the filling, whisk together ½ cup (120 ml) of the Key lime juice with the condensed milk, egg yolks, and salt. Pour the mixture into the crust and bake it for 20 to 25 minutes, or until the filling is set. Allow it to cool completely.

3. In the bowl of a stand mixer fitted with the whisk attachment, beat together the mascarpone, cream, confectioners' sugar, and remaining Key lime juice until the cream holds stiff peaks. Transfer the cream to a pastry bag fitted with a decorative tip and pipe it onto the cooled Key lime pie.

OH NUTS!

I SEE A PECAN PIE, AND BEFORE ANYONE THINKS ABOUT ASKING ME IF I WANT A SLICE, I MAKE IT VERY CLEAR THAT I'M GOING TO BE PARTAKING BY BOLDLY DECLARING, "YES, PLEASE!" I say this loudly, and I fix a loopy grin on my face, the kind of smile that's slightly off and screams, "Don't look that lady in the eye! She's touched and possibly dangerous." The guarantee that comes with this open declaration and attendant loopy face is that no matter what the intended future for that pie, at least one slice of it will be mine.

Classic
PECAN PIE

Quick Puff Pastry (page 22)	⅛ batch	
unsalted butter	½ cup	115 g
light brown sugar, firmly packed	1½ cups	330 g
light corn syrup	¾ cup	180 ml
vanilla bean paste	1 tablespoon	15 ml
salt	1 teaspoon	6 g
eggs	4	
pecan pieces, lightly toasted	1½ cups	165 g
pecan halves	½ cup	50 g

MAKES 1
(9-INCH/23-CM) PIE

1. Preheat the oven to 350°F (175°C). Roll out the dough into a rough 11-inch (28-cm) circle. Line a 9-inch (23-cm) pie plate with the dough, crimp the edges decoratively, and dock the bottom. Freeze the crust for 20 minutes. Line the crust with parchment, fill it with pie weights or dried beans, and bake it for 15 minutes. Remove the weights and parchment and bake the crust for 5 minutes more, or just until the bottom loses its raw-dough sheen. Do not let the crust brown. Set it aside.

2. In a heavy saucepan, melt the butter over low heat. Add the brown sugar and stir until the sugar has melted and all the lumps are gone. Add the corn syrup, vanilla, and salt, and stir until combined.

3. In a mixing bowl, whisk together the eggs. Whisking briskly, ladle about ½ cup (120 ml) of the hot sugar syrup into the eggs. This tempers the eggs, bringing their temperature closer to that of the hot syrup and preventing them from scrambling. Pour the egg mixture into the saucepan, whisking all the while. Keep whisking until the eggs are completely integrated.

4. Stir in the pecan pieces and pour the mixture into the piecrust. Arrange the pecan halves decoratively on top of the filling. Bake for 50 minutes to 1 hour, or just until the filling has set.

NOTE
By replacing the Quick Puff with Sweet Tart Dough (page 30), you can have a pecan tart that's reminiscent of a candy bar. Absolutely and sinfully delicious. And you don't need to be constrained to pecans, either. Walnuts, almonds, macadamia nuts . . . all manner of nuts are perfectly acceptable replacements. Or mix them all up for a nutty party!

Nutella Tart

Classic Pecan Pie

I COULDN'T BELIEVE MY LUCK WHEN NUTELLA APPEARED AT THE *BREAKFAST* TABLE IN MY TANTE CHRISTEL'S VACATION HOME IN GERMANY. I thought surely the adults had no idea that they were serving a chocolate spread during the most important meal of the day. I slathered the stuff on top of a crusty piece of bread already heavily layered with sweet cream butter and scarfed it quickly before my mother figured out what the hell was going into my mouth.

Today, I keep an economy-size jar in my pantry and sneak spoonfuls when no one's looking. It's not like anyone can stop me; after all, I'm a big girl now. But there's so much pleasure in that small mouthful of chocolate and hazelnut that it has to be wrong, even though it tastes so right. In this tart, I create the telltale Nutella flavor from gianduja chocolate, a hazelnut-infused chocolate. It's available at high-end grocery stores or online.

MAKES 1
(9-INCH/23-CM) TART

Chocolate Cookie Tart Crust (page 31)	½ batch	
gianduja chocolate, chopped (I use Callebaut)	10 ounces	280 g
semisweet chocolate, chopped (I use Callebaut's 60/40)	10 ounces	280 g
heavy cream	2 cups	480 ml
unsalted butter	4 tablespoons	55 g
salt	¼ teaspoon	1.5 g
vanilla bean paste	1 teaspoon	5 ml
chopped, roasted hazelnuts	1 cup	115 g

1. Preheat the oven to 350°F (175°C). Line a 9-inch (23-cm) tart pan with the dough and cut the excess from the edges. Dock the dough and freeze it for 20 minutes. Line the crust with parchment, fill it with pie weights or dried beans, and bake it for 15 minutes. Remove the parchment and pie weights and bake the crust for 15 minutes more, or until it is baked through. Set it aside to cool completely.

2. Place the gianduja and semisweet chocolates in a large, heatproof mixing bowl. In a saucepan, bring the cream, butter, salt, and vanilla to a simmer. Pour the cream mixture into the bowl with the chocolate and allow it to sit undisturbed for 5 minutes. Whisk the mixture until all the chocolate has melted and it is smooth.

3. Pour the chocolate filling into the prepared crust. Refrigerate the tart until it is partially set, about 20 minutes. Sprinkle the chopped hazelnuts along the edge of the tart, then return it to the refrigerator until it is completely set, about 1 hour more.

HAZELNUT TART

MAKES 1
(8- OR 9-INCH/20- OR 23-CM) PIE

HAZELNUTS—OR FILBERTS, FOR THOSE WITH A NEED TO EXPAND THEIR CULINARY VOCABULARY—ARE BUTTERY AND ELEGANT. This is a perfect and surprising alternative to the classic pecan pie for your Thanksgiving table.

FOR THE CRUST		
Sweet Tart Dough (page 30), Hazelnut option	½ batch	
FOR THE FILLING		
unsalted butter	4 tablespoons	55 g
dark brown sugar, firmly packed	¾ cup	165 g
maple syrup	¼ cup	60 ml
light corn syrup	¼ cup	60 ml
vanilla bean paste	1 teaspoon	5 ml
salt	½ teaspoon	3 g
eggs	2	
hazelnuts, chopped and roasted	1 cup	115 g
FOR THE ASSEMBLY		
Clear Caramel for Glazing (page 36), prepared through step 2	1 batch	
whole hazelnuts, toasted, with the skins rubbed off	1 cup	135 g

Procedure for the crust

Preheat the oven to 350°F (175°C). Line an 8- or 9-inch (20- or 23-cm) tart pan with the dough, then dock the dough and freeze it for 20 minutes. Line the crust with parchment, fill it with pie weights or dried beans, and bake it for 15 minutes. Remove the pie weights and parchment and bake the crust for 5 minutes more, or just until the bottom loses its raw-dough sheen—it shouldn't be at all browned. Set the crust aside.

Procedure for the filling

1. In a heavy saucepan, melt the butter over low heat. Add the brown sugar and stir until it is melted and there are no more sugar lumps. Add the maple syrup, corn syrup, vanilla, and salt. Stir until just combined.

2. In a separate bowl, whisk the eggs. Ladle a small portion of the hot sugar syrup into the eggs, whisking all the while. This tempers the eggs, bringing their temperature closer to that of the sugar syrup and preventing them from scrambling. Pour the egg mixture into the saucepan, stirring constantly. Add the hazelnuts and stir vigorously.

3. Pour the mixture into the crust and bake it for 20 to 30 minutes, or until the filling is set. Allow the tart to cool completely.

Assembly

1. To make the caramel-coated hazelnuts, fill a large bowl with ice and set it aside. Lay a sheet of parchment out on the counter.

2. Prepare the caramel as instructed on page 36. After finishing step 2, transfer the pot directly from the heat to the bowl of ice to cool it quickly (don't let any ice or water jump into the pot with the caramel).

3. Before the caramel sets, add the whole hazelnuts to the pot and stir gently. Remove the hazelnuts one by one with a *clean* pair of tweezers (I have a pair dedicated to kitchen use) and place them on the parchment so that they do not touch. Let them sit until they have cooled and hardened, then arrange them decoratively on top of the tart.

LINZER
Torte

MAKES 1
(12-INCH/30.5-CM) TART

unsalted butter	1½ cups	340 g
sugar	2 cups	400 g
eggs	2	
all-purpose flour	2 cups	250 g
ground hazelnuts	12 ounces	340 g
orange zest	1 teaspoon	2 g
cinnamon	1 teaspoon	3 g
ground cloves	½ teaspoon	1.5 g
salt	1 teaspoon	6 g
lingonberry preserves	1½ cups	360 ml

1. Preheat the oven to 325°F (165°C). Lightly coat the inside of a 12-inch (30.5-cm) tart pan or cake ring with nonstick cooking spray.

2. In the bowl of a stand mixer fitted with the paddle attachment, cream together the butter and sugar. Add the eggs, one at a time, beating well after each addition to ensure that it is completely incorporated. In another large bowl, whisk together the flour, hazelnuts, zest, cinnamon, cloves, and salt. Slowly add the flour mixture to the egg mixture and beat until just combined.

3. Transfer a little more than half of the dough to a large pastry bag fitted with a large open tip. Pipe the dough in concentric circles inside the prepared tart pan or cake ring, positioning the circles close together so that they touch and form a solid round base. Bake the crust for 20 minutes, or just until it begins to brown. Allow it to cool slightly.

4. Spread the lingonberry preserves in an even layer over the crust. Transfer the remaining dough to the pastry bag and pipe parallel lines ½ inch (12 mm) apart across the surface of the tart. Pipe another set of parallel lines perpendicular to the first set to create a lattice pattern. With the remaining batter, pipe dots along the perimeter to create a border.

5. Bake the torte for 30 minutes, or just until the pastry begins to brown. Cool it completely before serving.

MONT BLANC IS THE HIGHEST MOUNTAIN IN THE ALPS AND IS ALSO A WELL-KNOWN TART, PILED HIGH WITH CHEST-NUT PUREE, WHICH IS MEANT TO REPRESENT THE LOFT AND GRANDEUR OF THE PEAK. Somehow, a winding pile of soft brown nut strands hardly stands a chance of embodying the white-capped, craggy stone grandeur of Mont Blanc. Instead of recreating the Alpine spire delicacy, I've turned my sights to my home state of Vermont in an attempt to honor her mountain's majesty in pastry as the French have done—but I think I have an easier task than my European colleagues. Our fair state is known for her green mountains, and that's easy enough to recreate with my all-time favorite nut, the pistachio. So I'm happy to say that the Mont Pelier, named after our state capital, is both highly representative of our lovely peaks and also delicious!

This recipe will make more than the ten meringues required for the Mont Pelier. I usually end up with fourteen or fifteen. Take advantage of this and pipe all the meringue into pretty mounds. You'll find that not every mountain of meringue is equal—a couple will be lopsided, and a couple will be squat. This way, you can pick and choose! I also use the uglier piles as testers, pulling them out of the oven to check for doneness. It's win-win all around.

MONT PELIER Tartlets

MAKES 10
(4-INCH/10-CM) TARTLETS

NOTE
If you cannot get your hands on pistachio flour (I get mine through Nutsonline.com), pulse together 2 cups (245 g) whole pistachios with ¼ cup (50 g) granulated sugar until a fine nut meal forms. Take care not to overmix; otherwise, the mixture will turn into a paste.

FOR THE CRUSTS		
Sweet Tart Dough (page 30)	1 batch	
FOR THE MERINGUES		
egg whites	½ cup	120 ml
blackberry puree	2 tablespoons	30 ml
lemon juice	1 drop	
salt	pinch	
sugar	1 cup	200 g
FOR THE PISTACHIO COVERING		
pistachio nut paste (I use Love'n Bake brand)	2 (11-ounce) cans	2 (312-g) cans
almond paste (I use Odense brand)	2 (7-ounce) packages	2 (198-g) packages
confectioners' sugar, if needed	up to ½ cup	up to 50 g
FOR THE ASSEMBLY		
blackberry preserves	1 cup	240 ml
pistachio flour (see Note)	2 cups	225 g
fresh blackberries or pomegranate kernels, for decorating		

Procedure for the crusts

Preheat the oven to 325°F (165°C). Line 10 (4-inch/10-cm) flan tart rings with dough. Dock the crusts and freeze them for 20 minutes. Line the crusts with parchment, fill them with pie weights or dried beans, and bake them for 15 minutes. Remove the pie weights and parchment, and bake the crusts for 10 minutes more, or until they are baked through.

Procedure for the meringues

1. Reduce the oven temperature to 220°F (105°C). In the bowl of a stand mixer fitted with the whisk attachment, beat together the egg whites, blackberry puree, lemon juice, and salt until foamy and thick (but not dry). With the mixer on high, slowly add the sugar. This should take a few minutes—be patient. The very slow incorporation of the sugar is the key to preventing your meringues from weeping. Whisk until you achieve stiff, shiny white peaks.

2. Transfer the meringue to a large pastry bag fitted with a large star tip. Pipe 2½- to 3-inch-tall (6- to 7.5-cm-tall) mounds approximately 1½ to 2 inches (4 to 5 cm) wide at the base onto a baking sheet lined with parchment. Bake them for about 1½ hours, or until just dry. Allow them to cool completely.

Procedure for the pistachio covering

Place the pistachio and almond pastes in the bowl of a food processor and pulse until they are combined. You may need to add a few table-spoons of confectioners' sugar to counteract the natural oiliness of the pistachio paste and create a suitably pliable mixture (rather the way pure almond paste naturally is)—add as needed and pulse until a smooth paste forms. Transfer the mixture to a small bowl and refrigerate.

Assembly

1. Divide the blackberry preserves among the crusts and spread them smooth with the back of a spoon. Choose the 10 prettiest meringues and place one in each tartlet.

2. Transfer the nut paste to a work surface lightly dusted with pistachio flour. Divide the paste into 10 even pieces, roll each into a foot-long (30.5-cm-long) strand, and wrap it around a meringue, pinching off any excess. Press gently so that the meringue is totally covered and there are no gaps that allow it to peek through. Coat the tartlet with more pistachio flour. Top it with a piece of blackberry or a pomegranate kernel. Serve immediately.

MACADAMIA-
Coconut-Caramel
TART

MAKES 1
(8-INCH/20-CM) TART

DO I HAVE TO EXPLAIN WHY CRUNCHY, BUTTERY, AND CHEWY ARE GOOD THINGS? This decadent tart is addictive and more than a little like a sophisticated candy bar. If you're at all greedy, don't tell anyone you've made this until you've gotten your fill. You'll thank me later.

FOR THE CRUST		
macadamia nuts, chopped	1 cup	132 g
all-purpose flour	1½ cups	185 g
salt	1 teaspoon	6 g
sugar	⅓ cup	65 g
unsalted butter, chilled and cut into small pieces	½ cup	115 g
whole egg	1	60 ml
vanilla bean paste	1 teaspoon	5 ml
FOR THE CARAMEL	**1 TEASPOON**	**5 ML**
sugar	¼ cup	50g
light corn syrup	2 tablespoons	30 ml
salt	pinch	115 g
heavy cream	2 tablespoons	30 ml
unsalted butter	1 tablespoon	14 g
FOR THE ASSEMBLY		
sweetened coconut flakes	1 cup	85 g
Pastry Cream (page 35), prepared with coconut milk instead of whole milk and with only a pinch of salt	1 batch	

Procedure for the crust

1. In the bowl of a food processor, pulse together the macadamia nuts, flour, salt, and sugar. Add the butter, and continue pulsing until the mixture looks like coarse cornmeal. In a small bowl, whisk together the egg and vanilla. Pour the mixture into the processor and pulse until the dough just comes together. Turn the dough out onto a piece of plastic wrap. Shape it into a loose disk, cover it entirely with plastic wrap, and refrigerate it for 30 minutes.

2. Press the dough into a fluted 8-inch (20-cm) tart pan, forming an even layer. Allow it to rest in the freezer for 30 minutes.

3. Preheat the oven to 325°F (165°C). Line the crust with parchment and fill it with pie weights or dried beans. Bake the crust for 20 to 30 minutes, until it is lightly golden brown and baked through. Allow it to cool completely.

Procedure for the caramel

1. In a large saucepan, combine the sugar, corn syrup, salt, and 2 table-spoons (30 ml) water and stir the mixture over low heat until the sugar crystals completely dissolve. Wash any errant sugar crystals down the sides of the pan using a damp pastry brush. Stop stirring and clip on a candy thermometer. Heat the syrup to 245°F (120°C).

2. Once the syrup has reached temperature, carefully add the cream and butter. The mixture will bubble vigorously at first. Step back and let the hot sugar do its molten dance. When it has stopped bubbling, stir the caramel until the butter and cream are completely incorporated. Pour it into the crust, spreading it with a small offset spatula or the back of a spoon to make sure that the entire bottom is coated. Refrigerate the tart until set, at least 30 minutes.

Assembly

1. Spread the coconut flakes on a baking sheet and toast them in a 325°F (165°C) oven until they are fragrant and lightly brown. Set them aside to cool completely.

2. Prepare the coconut pastry cream. Once it has cooled, stir it until it loosens and becomes smooth (it will have thickened considerably in the refrigerator), then spoon it over the caramel. Spread it evenly with a small offset spatula.

3. Sprinkle the coconut over the pastry cream in an even layer so that it covers the top of the tart completely. Serve immediately.

STRUDELS

IT'S THE DESSERT STAPLE OF SO MANY—SWEET LAYERS OF
CRISPY DOUGH SATURATED WITH HONEY AND GRACED WITH
NUTS. It's a more delicate version of pecan pie, and definitely more
flaky, pure in its simplicity and surprisingly satisfying.

BAKLAVA

shelled pistachios	1 pound	455 g
cinnamon	1 teaspoon	3 g
Strudel Dough (page 31), stretched and brushed with butter	1 batch	
unsalted butter, melted	1 cup	225 g
sugar	1 cup	200 g
vanilla extract	1 teaspoon	5 ml
honey	½ cup	120 ml
orange zest	1 tablespoon	6 g
salt	¼ teaspoon	1.5 g

MAKES 1
(8-BY-12-INCH/20-BY-30.5-CM)
PASTRY

1. Preheat the oven to 350°F (175°C). Line a 9-by-13-inch (23-by-33-cm) baking sheet with parchment; coat it with nonstick cooking spray.

2. In the bowl of a food processor, pulse together the pistachios and cinnamon until finely ground. Set the mixture aside.

3. Trim the butter-brushed strudel dough into pieces slightly smaller than your baking sheet. Place 2 sheets of strudel dough on top of each other on the baking sheet and brush the entire surface with more melted butter. Continue layering the dough 2 sheets at a time and then buttering, until you have 8 sheets; sprinkle ¼ cup (60 ml) of the nut mixture over the top layer. Repeat until you have used all of your dough sheets. The top layer should have at least 6 sheets of dough.

4. Using a straight-edge ruler as a guide, cut the dough lengthwise and crosswise with a large, sharp serrated knife every 3 inches (7.5 cm), so you'll have 12 pieces of baklava. Make sure you cut all the way through, cleanly, to the bottom layers. Bake for 45 to 50 minutes, until the baklava is golden brown and the top layer is crisp.

5. While the baklava is baking, in a heavy saucepan, bring the sugar and 1 cup (240 ml) water to a boil. When the sugar is melted, add the vanilla, honey, zest, and salt, and simmer for about 20 minutes.

6. Remove the baklava from the oven and immediately spoon the sauce over it. Cool it completely before serving.

APFEL-STRUDEL

MAKES 1
(4-BY-12-INCH/10-BY-30.5-CM)
STRUDEL

THIS STRUDEL IS TERRIBLY SIMPLE, WHICH IS PERFECT SINCE YOU'VE GONE THROUGH SO MUCH WORK TO STRETCH THE DOUGH. You deserve a quick and delicious pastry as a reward!

FOR THE FILLING		
apples, cored and cut into ½-inch (12 mm) cubes	4	
raisins	1 cup	145 g
rum	2 tablespoons	30 ml
zest and juice of 1 lemon		
brown sugar, firmly packed	½ cup	110 g
all-purpose flour	3 tablespoons	22 g
salt	pinch	165 g
FOR THE ASSEMBLY		
walnuts, very finely chopped (optional)	1 cup	120 g
Strudel Dough (page 31), stretched and brushed with butter	1 batch	
unsalted butter, melted	4 tablespoons	55 g
confectioners' sugar, for sprinkling	¼ cup	25 g

Procedure for the filling

In a large bowl, toss the apples, raisins, rum, and lemon zest and juice. In a small bowl, whisk together the brown sugar, flour, and salt, and sprinkle this over the apple mixture. Toss until the apples are evenly coated.

Assembly

1. Preheat the oven to 350°F (175°C). Line a baking sheet with parchment.

2. If you are including walnuts, sprinkle them evenly over the entire surface of the dough. The butter will help the walnuts stick. Spoon the apples onto the narrow end of the long stretch of dough, leaving a hand's width of dough uncovered on either side of the filling. Take hold of the tablecloth upon which your dough is sitting and lift it to flip the dough and the filling end over end, wrapping the filling tightly in the dough. (*Strudel* means "whirlpool," and the pastry is so named because of this wrapping motion.) Once you've rolled up all the dough, trim the sides of extraneous dough, leaving enough to tuck under the strudel.

3. Transfer the strudel to the baking sheet and brush it with the melted butter. Bake it for 40 to 45 minutes, or until it is golden brown. Allow the strudel to cool completely and then sift confectioners' sugar over the top to finish.

THIS CREAMY PASTRY IS ONE OF MY CHILDHOOD FAVORITES. It is marvelously refreshing, despite the fact that is filled with fresh farmer's cheese. And don't let the idea of farmer's cheese turn you off of this most delicious of desserts; it's light and sumptuous and takes flavor beautifully.

CHEESE
STRUDEL
(Topfenstrudel)

FOR THE FILLING		
eggs	3	
quark, farmer's cheese, or ricotta cheese	1 pound	455 g
unsalted butter, softened	6 tablespoons	85 g
sultana raisins	1 cup	145 g
dried apricots, diced	1 cup	130 g
zest and juice of 1 lemon		
sugar	⅔ cup	130 g
salt	½ teaspoon	3 g
vanilla bean paste	1 teaspoon	5 ml
FOR THE ASSEMBLY		
Strudel Dough (page 31), stretched and brushed with butter	1 batch	
unsalted butter, melted	4 tablespoons	55 g
confectioners' sugar, for sprinkling	¼ cup	25 g

MAKES 1
(6-BY-12-INCH/15-BY-30.5-CM)
STRUDEL

Procedure for the filling

In a large bowl, whisk the eggs. Add the cheese and butter and stir until completely combined. Add the raisins, apricots, lemon zest and juice, sugar, salt, and vanilla, and stir until well combined.

Assembly

1. Preheat the oven to 350°F (175°C). Line a large baking sheet with parchment.

2. Spoon the filling onto the narrow end of the long stretch of butter-brushed dough, leaving a hand's width of dough uncovered on either side of the filling. Take hold of the tablecloth upon which your dough is sitting, and lift it to flip the dough and the filling end over end, wrapping the filling tightly in the dough. Once you've rolled up all the dough, trim the sides of extraneous dough, but leave enough to tuck under the strudel.

3. Transfer the strudel to the baking sheet and brush with the melted butter. Bake it for 40 to 45 minutes, or until it is golden brown. Allow the strudel to cool completely and then sift confectioners' sugar over it.

LOBSTER TAILS

MAKES 8-10
PASTRIES

IF YOU'VE EVER BEEN TO BOSTON'S NORTH END AND YOU HAVEN'T HAD A LOBSTER TAIL, OR *SFOGLIATELLE*, THEN YOU HAVEN'T BEEN TO BOSTON'S NORTH END. These delicious and super-cool-looking treats are an Italian tradition that have become Boston staples and should be a regular feature on your family's menu.

egg, beaten	1	
heavy cream	1 cup	240 ml
ricotta cheese	1½ cups	360 ml
semolina flour	¼ cup	30 g
sugar	⅓ cup	65 g
vanilla bean paste	1 teaspoon	5 ml
orange zest	1 tablespoon	6 g
cinnamon	¼ teaspoon	1 g
salt	½ teaspoon	3 g
Strudel Dough (page 31), stretched and brushed with butter (see Note)	1 batch	
unsalted butter, for your hands	2 tablespoons	28 g
confectioners' sugar, for sprinkling	¼ cup	25 g

1. In a large bowl, stir together the egg, cream, and cheese until completely combined. Add the flour, sugar, vanilla, zest, cinnamon, and salt and stir until well combined. Transfer the filling into a pastry bag fitted with a medium open tip and set it aside.

2. Preheat the oven to 350°F (175°C). Line 2 large baking sheets with parchment.

3. Using a very sharp knife, cut the butter-brushed dough lengthwise into 4 long, even strips. (See image A.) Starting at one end of a strip, roll the dough tightly, like a hand-rolled cigarette. Stretch as you work, but without tearing the dough. (See image B.) Once you've reached the end of the length of the first strip, transfer the dough roll to the next strip and continue rolling as if the line of dough hadn't been broken. Continue rolling the remaining dough onto the same dough roll until you have one big roll. Trim the rough edges and cut the roll into 1-inch (2.5-cm) rounds. (See image C.)

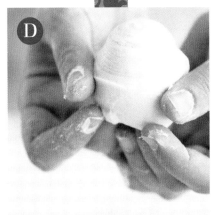

4. Rub your hands with a little butter. Pick up a round of dough and flatten it slightly with your palm. Using your thumbs, gently stretch the disk of dough to create a bowl, making sure to keep the strips of dough attached. (See image D.)

5. Pipe filling into the lobster tails and pinch the open ends to seal the pastries.

6. Place the lobster tails a little bit apart (they won't spread) on the prepared baking sheet. Bake them for 15 to 20 minutes, until the pastry is golden brown and flaky. Allow the *sfogliatelle* to cool completely before sprinkling them with confectioners' sugar.

NOTE

Traditionally, butter is used to brush the dough for these pastries. If you prefer, use 4 to 8 ounces (115 to 225 g) melted shortening to finish your strudel dough, instead of butter.

CHAPTER

3

the

SAVORIES

Pie doesn't have to be sweet. As a matter of fact, some of the first pies were savory "hot pockets" of traveling goodness filled with meats and such, which accompanied sailors and soldiers on long slogs. Savory pies may be elegant, like quiche, or they may be homey. Once you get a sense of what's possible in the savory pie world, dinner (and leftovers) will never be the same. If you've got a homemade piecrust in the oven and a semi-picked-apart turkey carcass in the fridge, you've got the makings of one of the best one-dish dinners in history.

Instead of giving you the standards here, I'm going to give you my own take on the world of savory pie. On a recent trip to England, during which my husband, Ray, and I undertook a pie crawl, I took to heart the variety and depth of flavor that can be found in a single concept. Pie in England has always been varied. In the early days, there really was no choice in the matter: Leftovers, scraps from all manner of meals, were commingled into one pie shell and baked to oblivion, the results of which were rarely edible. But you can take that concept, of a tasty shell just waiting for a filling, and run with it. I now have!

CORNISH
Pasties

MAKES 4
PASTIES

THIS IS THE "PASTY" OF CORNWALL, TRADITIONALLY FILLED WITH BEEF AND FORMED INTO A LITTLE HALF-MOON POCKET OF SUCCULENT YUMMYNESS. It's filled with potatoes *and* turnips, so it's meant to be very filling. If you want to be old-school, before baking the pasty, gently score it with the initials of the lucky little pie eaters who are going to get a pasty of their very own.

Part-Butter/Part-Shortening Easy Pie Dough (page 19)	1 batch	
beef tenderloin, cut into 4-inch (10-cm) square cubes	½ pound	225 g
flour	2 tablespoons	15 g
paprika	1 teaspoon	3 g
olive oil	1 tablespoon	15 ml
potato, peeled and cut into ¼-inch (6-mm) cubes	1	
sweet yellow onion, minced	1	
garlic, minced	2 cloves	
dried thyme	1 teaspoon	1 g
salt and pepper	to taste	
egg wash (1 egg whisked with 2 tablespoons/30 ml water)		

1. Cut the dough into 4 even pieces and roll each into an 8-inch (20-cm) round. Transfer to them to parchment-lined sheet pans.

2. Pat the beef pieces dry with a paper towel. Place them in a mixing bowl and sprinkle them with the flour and paprika. Toss to coat evenly.

3. In a large frying pan, heat the olive oil. Add the beef pieces in one layer and brown them evenly. Transfer them to a large bowl and allow them to come to room temperature.

4. When the beef has cooled, stir in the potato, onion, garlic, thyme, salt, and pepper.

5. Preheat the oven to 350°F (175°C). Brush each round of dough with egg wash. Divide the filling among the rounds, piling it in the middle of each round. Bring the sides of the dough up to meet in the middle and gently crimp the edges down the center. Cut 2 vent holes to allow steam to escape.

6. Brush the tops of the pasties with egg wash and bake for 45 minutes.

IF YOU'VE EVER COVERED A TABLE WITH NEWSPAPER AND DUMPED OUT THE CONTENTS OF A SPICY POT OF PIPING-HOT SUCCULENCE IN THE FORM OF A MESSY PILE OF SHRIMP, CORN, POTATOES, AND SAUSAGE, THEN YOU KNOW HOW DELICIOUS A SUMMER NIGHT IN LOUISIANA CAN BE. You also know how messy it gets. This fine pie gives you all the yummy without the need for cleanup.

FOR THE CRUST		
Easy Rustic Pie Dough (page 19)	½ batch	
FOR THE FILLING		
organic low-salt chicken broth	3 cups	720 ml
Cajun spice blend	1 teaspoon	2.5 g
cayenne	pinch	
unsalted butter	2 tablespoons	28 g
regular (not quick-cooking) grits	1 cup	155 g
Idaho potato	1	
sharp cheddar cheese, shredded	8 ounces	225 g
heavy cream	½ cup	120 ml
red bell pepper, chopped into a fine dice	1	
jalapeño pepper, deseeded and chopped	1	
fresh corn kernels (from 2 cobs)	1 cup	165 g
andouille sausage, casing removed, cut into small pieces	1 link	
eggs	4	
salt	to taste (see Note)	
fresh, raw medium-sized shrimp	½ pound	225 g

Procedure for the crust

Preheat the oven to 350°F (175°C). Line a 9-inch (23-cm) pie pan with the dough. Dock the dough and freeze it for 20 minutes. Line the crust with parchment, fill it with pie weights or dried beans, and bake it for 15 minutes. Remove the pie weights and parchment and bake the crust for 5 to 10 minutes more, just until the raw-dough sheen goes away. Set the crust aside.

Procedure for the filling

1. Bring the chicken broth, Cajun spice, cayenne, and butter to a boil in a large saucepan. Stir in the grits and whisk until combined. Reduce the heat to low and simmer until the grits thicken, 8 to 10 minutes.

Low-Country
BOIL
PIE

MAKES 1
(9-INCH/23-CM) PIE

NOTE
Cajun spice mixes are often very salty, so be sure to check the flavor of the grits prior to adding salt to make sure you're not overdoing it.

2. Peel the potato, place it in a small saucepan filled with water, and boil until it is fork-tender. Cool the potato and cut it into ½-inch (12-mm) cubes.

3. Add the cheddar, cream, bell pepper, jalapeño, corn, andouille, and potato to the grits and stir until combined.

4. In a small bowl, whisk the eggs to break them up and stir them into the grits. Test the seasoning and add salt to taste. Add the shrimp, stirring gently to distribute them evenly.

5. Pour the mixture into the crust. Bake the pie for 35 to 40 minutes, or until the custard is set.

A NOTE FROM THE SWEETIE PIE

"Fork-tender" is literal when it comes to testing the doneness of a potato. You use a fork to determine whether the flesh is tender because it takes some doing to get the fork through the skin into the middle. Now, if you use a paring knife or any other sharp knife, it will easily slip straight through into the meat whether the potato is actually fully tender or not. You're likely to have a false reading! So stick a fork in it, not a knife, to judge whether your potato is done.

Fried (Slightly) Green Tomato Tart

Low-Country Boil Pie

FRIED (Slightly) Green TOMATO Tart

MAKES 1
(10-INCH/25-CM) TART

NOTE

If you reside in northern climes, it's rare to see a green tomato (simply an unripe tomato) in your grocery store. So unless you grow your own, check for a tomato that's very firm to the touch, one you'd otherwise not purchase because it's not yet ripe.

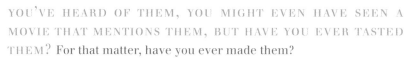For that matter, have you ever made them?

Well, let me tell you, fried green tomatoes are just as good as they sound. Probably better. Crispy on the outside, juicy and tender inside, they're a summertime treat. And once you sample them set atop a tender, savory, sconelike, free-form crust smothered in a light layer of pimento cheese spread (stay with me here), you'll be a convert to this underripe delicacy forevermore.

FOR THE TOMATOES		
finely ground cornmeal	½ cup	78 g
all-purpose flour	½ cup	60 g
Cajun or Creole spice blend (I like Emeril's)	½ teaspoon	1.2 g
salt	½ teaspoon	3 g
buttermilk	½ cup	120 ml
large, green tomatoes, cut into ½-inch-thick (12-mm-thick) slices, at room temperature	2	
vegetable oil	½ cup	120 ml
FOR THE CRUST		
all-purpose flour	1½ cups	185 g
finely ground cornmeal	½ cup	78 g
unsalted butter, chilled and cut into pieces	10 tablespoons	145 g
sugar	2 tablespoons	25 g
cayenne	½ teaspoon	1.5 g
salt	½ teaspoon	3 g
baking powder	1 tablespoon	15 g
tasso ham, cubed (you can substitute chorizo)	¼ pound	115 g
grated extra-sharp cheddar cheese	½ cup	60 g
buttermilk	½ cup	120 ml
egg	1	
FOR THE CHEESE SPREAD		
cornichons (tiny pickles)	4	
garlic	1 clove	
sharp cheddar cheese, finely grated	8 ounces	225 g
Monterey Jack cheese, finely grated	4 ounces	115 g
pimientos, juices drained	½ (4-ounce) jar	½ (113-g) jar
sour cream	¼ cup	60 ml
salt	½ teaspoon	3 g
hot sauce	2 drops	

Procedure for the tomatoes

1. In a large flat bowl, whisk together the cornmeal, flour, spice blend, and salt. Pour the buttermilk in a second bowl. Pat the tomato slices with a paper towel and dredge them in the flour mixture, then the buttermilk, and then back to the flour.

2. In a large frying pan, heat the oil to about 350°F (175°C) and fry the tomatoes on each side until golden brown. Place the finished slices on a grid-style cooling rack.

Procedure for the crust

1. Preheat the oven to 350°F (175°C). Line a baking sheet with parchment.

2. In a large mixing bowl, work the flour, cornmeal, butter, sugar, cayenne, salt, and baking powder with your fingers until the mixture resembles cornmeal and all of the butter is well incorporated. Add the ham and cheese and toss to distribute evenly.

3. In a small bowl, whisk together the buttermilk and egg. Add this to the dough and work the mixture gently with your hands until it is uniformly wet and no dry clumps of flour remain. *Don't overwork the dough.*

4. Scoop the dough onto the prepared baking sheet and gently press it into a rough 10-inch (25-cm) round. Bake until the crust is golden brown and baked through, 35 to 45 minutes. Allow it to cool.

Procedure for the cheese spread

Chop the cornichons and garlic into small pieces and place them in the bowl of a food processor, along with the cheeses, pimientos, sour cream, salt, and hot sauce. Process until smooth.

Assembly

Spread the pimento cheese in an even layer over the cooled crust. Arrange the tomatoes over the top of the spread, overlapping them if you have to. Serve the pie immediately.

A NOTE FROM THE SWEETIE PIE

When you're frying, as in the case of green tomatoes, it's crucial that the temperature of the oil remain steady; otherwise, the items you mean to make crispy and crunchy will simply come out soggy. It's also important that the food you're frying be at room temperature—you can't fry something straight from the fridge, or it'll draw the temperature of the oil too far down. Hence the direction that the tomatoes be at room temperature.

A QUICHE *For All* SEASONS

MAKES 1
(9-INCH/23-CM) PIE

IT'S SO DAMN SIMPLE, MAKING QUICHE. It's one of the best "kitchen-sink" recipes on earth, but it comes wrapped in such fancy French culinary esteem that you need only add "quiche" to the end of your creation and everyone at the dinner table will say "oooooh!" and then "ahhhhh!"

Quiche at its heart is a custard pie, its essential elements being heavy cream, milk, eggs, and seasoning (and usually a nice dose of cheese). If you keep the basic ratios of the custard in your head, you can throw in just about anything that's hanging out in your fridge.

Quick Puff Pastry (page 22)	⅛ batch	
lardon, cubed	6 ounces	170 g
heavy cream	1 cup	240 ml
whole milk	½ cup	120 ml
eggs	3	
salt	½ teaspoon	3 g
white pepper	½ teaspoon	1.5 g
nutmeg	pinch	
finely grated Gruyère cheese	1 cup	120 g

1. Preheat the oven to 350°F (175°C). Roll out the dough and use it to line a 9-inch (23-cm) pie plate. Dock the dough and freeze it for 20 minutes. Line the crust with parchment, fill it with pie weights or dried beans, and bake it for 15 minutes. Remove the pie weights and parchment and bake the crust for 5 minutes more, or just until the raw-dough sheen is gone. Set it aside.

2. In a heavy skillet, sauté the lardon cubes until they are crispy and the fat is rendered. Transfer them to a plate lined with a paper towel.

3. In a large bowl, whisk together the cream, milk, eggs, salt, pepper, and nutmeg. Stir in the cheese and the lardon, and pour the filling into the crust.

4. Bake the quiche for 30 minutes, or until the filling begins to puff and turns golden brown.

OPTIONS!

As I've said, this is a kitchen-sink recipe. The base formula for the filling is 1 cup (240 ml) cream, ½ cup (120 ml) milk, and 3 eggs. Then you can add whatever you like.

Option 1

Who doesn't have a half-eaten package of smoked salmon sitting around in the meat drawer? I know I do! Add some sautéed red pepper and onion, a spoonful of minced fresh dill, and some salt and pepper. Stir in your favorite cheese—a goat cheese would be lovely with that salmon—and voilà! You've got brunch.

Option 2

How about a Mexican quiche? Got some salsa? A bit of Manchego or Jack cheese? Jalapeño and chorizo? Perhaps finish with a chilled slice of avocado? Make with a cornmeal crust (page 19, option 2, and you've got a south-of-the-boarder delight.

Option 3

Or how about a Vermont special? Use some turkey and cheddar—and a few dried cranberries along for the ride.

PORK PIES

MAKES 8

(4-INCH/10-CM) INDIVIDUAL PORK PIES

I'VE NEVER MET A PORK PIE I DIDN'T LIKE. Culinarily inclined English folk and Anglophile Americans have sniffed at my porky exuberance: "Good pork pies are few and far between, unless you get a genuine Melton Mowbray (the home of great pork pies)," they say. I can't claim any such particularity. If it's pork in a pastry, I'm in. Whole hog.

But for you, I'm pulling out all the stops. To keep the juices locked into these individual beauties, I'm forgoing the traditional addition of aspic (meat Jell-O) to line the inside of the pastry and instead using prosciutto to provide a thin juice boundary keeping everything inside moist and tender and at the same time protecting the crust so it remains flaky. And instead of the super traditional hot-water pastry in which pork is commonly baked—providing a totally serviceable, though bland, container—I'm throwing caution to the wind and breaking out the buttery puff. Oh, heavens above, I'll have you eating pork pie weekly by the end of this. Serve these with a jar of cornichons (tiny pickles) and a small bowl of English mustard.

FOR THE CRUST		
Traditional Puff Pastry (page 25)	¼ batch	
FOR THE FILLING		
ground pork shoulder	1 pound	455 g
thick slab bacon, diced into ¼-inch (6-mm) cubes	1 pound	455 g
Worcestershire sauce	4 tablespoons	60 ml
wholegrain mustard	2 tablespoons	30 ml
salt	2 teaspoons	12 g
ground white pepper	1 teaspoon	3 g
dried thyme	1 teaspoon	1 g
anchovy paste	1 teaspoon	5 ml
orange zest	1 tablespoon	6 g
FOR THE ASSEMBLY		
egg wash (1 egg whisked with 2 tablespoons/30 ml water)		
large-flake fleur de sel (sea salt)	1 teaspoon	5 g
cornichons and mustard, for serving		

Procedure for the crust

1. Preheat the oven to 375°F (190°C). Roll the dough into an oblong shape between ⅛ and ¼ inch (3 and 6 mm) thick. Cut 8 (6-inch/15-cm) rounds from the dough to line small cake rings or the holes of a muffin tin. Cut

8 (3-inch/7.5-cm) rounds for the tops. Place the tops on a parchment-lined sheet pan, stamp a ¼-inch (6-mm) hole in the middle of each, cover them with plastic wrap, and refrigerate.

2. If you're using cake rings, place them on a parchment-lined sheet pan and line them with the larger-size dough rounds. If you're using a 12-hole muffin tin, first line 8 of the holes with strips of parchment 4 inches (10 cm) tall—the parchment will project above the top of the tin. Line those holes with the dough so that the parchment acts as a skirt around the outside. Tie a piece of butcher's twine around the parchment to keep the dough standing up straight. Dock the dough and freeze the crusts for 20 minutes.

3. Line each crust with parchment and fill it with pie weights or dried beans. Bake the crusts for 15 minutes. Remove the parchment and weights, and bake them for 5 to 10 minutes more, or until the crusts no longer have a raw-dough sheen. Allow the crusts to cool.

Procedure for the filling

In the bowl of a food processor fitted with the blade attachment, place half of the ground pork and half of the chopped bacon, along with the Worcestershire, mustard, salt, pepper, thyme, and anchovy paste. Pulse until the mass is well combined. Transfer the seasoned pork to a bowl along with the remaining pork and bacon. Blend the filling with your hands until it is well combined. Cover the bowl with plastic wrap and refrigerate it.

Assembly

1. Preheat the oven to 400°F (205°C). Line the bottom and sides of each crust with 2 pieces of prosciutto. Divide the filling evenly, place a top on each pie, and press gently to seal the edges. Brush the top of each pie with egg wash and sprinkle it with sea salt.

2. Bake the pies for 20 minutes and then reduce the heat to 350°F (175°C); bake them for 45 minutes more.

3. Allow the pies to cool enough that you can handle the cake rings or muffin tin. Gently remove the pies from the rings by pressing on the bottoms to pop them out. To remove them from the muffin tins, use a small offset spatula to gently pry the little pies from the tins.

4. Serve the pork pies warm or at room temperature, with cornichons and mustard.

NOTE

Before cutting the smaller rounds, you may need to gather up the pieces of dough and roll them out again. If so, make sure to stack the pieces one on top of the other to keep the layer structure, instead of just mushing everything together. Wrap the stacked scraps in plastic and refrigerate them for 20 minutes before rolling them out again.

CHICKEN POTPIES

MAKES 8
(4-INCH/10-CM) POTPIES

WHEN I WAS A KID, I WAS NEVER ALLOWED TO EAT ANY-THING REMOTELY POTPIE-ESQUE. So when I was old enough to take command of my own kitchen, I made it my mission to get my culinary fill of all manner of comfort food I'd been missing in my childhood. Chicken potpie was on the tippy-top of the list (along with Fanny Farmer's macaroni and cheese).

I prefer to use two different crusts, a buttery one on the bottom and a biscuit type for the top, to give the potpie texture and interest.

FOR THE BOTTOM CRUST		
Quick Puff Pastry (page 22)	½ batch	
FOR THE FILLING		
unsalted butter	2 tablespoons	28 g
olive oil	2 tablespoons	30 g
red bell pepper, seeded and finely chopped	1	
medium yellow onion, finely chopped	1	
large carrot, finely chopped	1	
garlic, minced	2 cloves	
fresh English peas or shelled broad beans (also known as fava beans)	2 cups	290 g
fresh corn kernels (from about 2 cobs)	1 cup	165 g
dried thyme	1 teaspoon	1 g
all-purpose flour	¼ cup	30 g
chicken broth	2 cups	480 ml
heavy cream	½ cup	120 ml
rotisserie chicken, meat picked off and set aside (about 2 cups' worth of meat)	1	
salt and pepper	to taste	
FOR THE TOP CRUST		
all-purpose flour	3 cups	375 g
salt	½ teaspoon	3 g
sugar	1 tablespoon	11 g
baking powder	1 tablespoon	15 g
vegetable shortening, frozen	½ cup	100 g
unsalted butter, chilled and cut into small pieces	½ cup	115 g
low-fat buttermilk	1 cup	240 ml
egg	1	
FOR THE ASSEMBLY		
egg wash (1 egg whisked with 2 tablespoons/30 ml water)		
coarse sea salt, for sprinkling		

Chicken Potpies

Pork Pies

Procedure for the bottom crust

Preheat the oven to 350°F (175°C). Divide the dough into 8 even pieces. Roll each piece into a rough round and use these to line 8 ramekins, letting them drape over the edges a little if they're big enough. Dock the bottoms and freeze them for 20 minutes. Line the crusts with parchment, fill them with pie weights or dried beans, and bake them for 20 minutes. Set them aside.

Procedure for the filling

1. In a large saucepan, melt the butter and olive oil over medium heat. Add the bell pepper, onion, carrot, and garlic and sauté until soft.

2. Stir in the peas, corn, and thyme. Sprinkle the flour over the vegetables and then add the chicken broth and cream. Stir to distribute the flour and the liquids. Simmer until the sauce thickens, about 10 minutes. Stir in the chicken and add salt and pepper to taste. Set the mixture aside to cool slightly.

Procedure for the top crust

1. In the bowl of a food processor, combine the flour, salt, sugar, and baking powder. Pulse a few times. Add the shortening and butter; pulse until the mixture resembles coarse cornmeal.

2. In a small bowl, whisk together the buttermilk and egg, and add this to the flour mixture. Pulse until the dough just comes together.

3. Turn the dough onto a floured work surface and knead gently until it just holds together. Pat it into a rough 8-by-16-inch (20-by-40.5-cm) rectangle and cut it into 8 (4-inch/10-cm) square pieces. (I cut the biscuit dough with a very sharp knife and trim the sides so the biscuits rise evenly and very high. By cutting them square, you waste little dough, and the shape provides visual interest against the round ramekin.)

4. Raise the oven temperature to 400°F (205°C).

Assembly

Remove the pie weights and parchment from the crusts and divide the filling evenly among them, filling just to the top. Top each filled ramekin with a square of biscuit dough. Brush the tops with the egg wash and sprinkle them with the sea salt. Bake the potpies for 20 minutes, until the filling is bubbling and the biscuits are golden brown.

OPTIONS!

Option 1 **Thanksgiving Potpie**

We always have plenty of turkey left over for a lovely batch of potpies. Most often I also have a fair bit of gravy and mashed potatoes. Proceed with the bottom crust as instructed for Chicken Potpies. Sauté the vegetables, decrease the cream to ¼ cup (60 ml), and add leftover gravy—¼ to ½ cup (60 to 120 ml) is perfect—to the mix. Top the potpies with mashed potatoes instead of the biscuit dough and bake them until the filling is bubbling.

Option 2 **Lobster Potpie**

If you are one of the lucky ducks who has access to fresh lobster, as we do in New England, it's rather easy to find a joint that will cook a lobster for you. (I'm too much of a wuss to cook my own.) Follow the recipe for Chicken Potpies, swapping 1 pound (455 g) lobster meat for the chicken and 2 cups (480 ml) fish broth or clam juice for the chicken broth.

Option 3 **Thai Green-Curry Potpie**

Substitute 1 cup (240 ml) coconut milk for an equal amount of the chicken broth and add 2 tablespoons (30 ml) green-curry paste in place of the thyme. You may want to emphasize vegetables like green and red bell peppers and larger pieces of onion. For the top crust, add 1 tablespoon (6 g) minced Thai basil to the biscuit dough to infuse the Thai flavor throughout the dish.

A Very Good
PIZZA
PIE

MAKES 1
(10-INCH/25-CM) PIE

I DREAM OF A PIZZA, ONE THAT I HAD SITTING AT THE BAR OF PANE E SALUTE IN WOODSTOCK, VERMONT. A slip of a pizza pie, thin and delicate, was our appetizer. To share. After my first bite, I was wallowing in regret. Why, oh why, hadn't I ordered one for myself with strict instructions to set it far, far away from my husband? Why did I have to parcel out pieces to him when I was capable of eating the entire thing myself?

Pizza Dough (page 33), on a peel as directed	1 batch	
extra-virgin olive oil, divided	3 tablespoons	45 ml
sweet yellow onion, cut into very thin strips	1	
garlic, minced	2 cloves	
fresh thyme, finely chopped	1 teaspoon	2 g
honey	1 teaspoon	5 ml
whole organic mandarin orange, skin still on, cut into very thin slices	1	
prosciutto, torn into large pieces	4 to 6 slices	
Taleggio cheese, finely grated or cubed	3 ounces	85 g
Parmigiano-Reggiano cheese, finely grated	¼ cup	25 g
salt and pepper	to taste	

1. Preheat the oven to 425°F (220°C) and place a pizza stone on the bottom rack. (See Note on page 33.)

2. In a large saucepan, heat 2 tablespoons (30 ml) of the olive oil over medium-low heat. Add the onion, garlic, thyme, and honey and sauté until the onion and garlic are very soft and just caramelized. Add the orange slices and sauté for 1 minute more.

3. Spread the remaining 1 tablespoon (15 ml) olive oil over the dough with the back of a spoon or your hands. Sprinkle the dough with the onion/garlic mixture, then pick out the orange slices so you can distribute them evenly atop the onions and garlic.

4. Drape the prosciutto across the dough and sprinkle the cheeses evenly over all. Use the peel to transfer the pie to the baking stone and bake for 20 minutes, or until the cheese is melted and the crust is golden brown. Sprinkle with salt and pepper to taste.

IN VERMONT, YOU CAN WALK INTO A SANDWICH SHOP WITH YOUR EYES CLOSED AND ORDER A VERMONTER. Go ahead, try it. You'll get a sandwich filled with Vermont cheddar, laced with sliced apples, loaded with turkey, often studded with bacon, and accompanied by a condiment, most often an aioli, that is dotted with cranberries and doused with a lick of maple syrup. It's delicious. It's even better as a pizza.

Vermonter's
PIZZA
PIE

MAKES 1
(10-INCH/25-CM) PIE

Pizza Dough (page 33), on a peel as directed	1 batch	
olive oil, divided	3 tablespoons	45 ml
sweet yellow onion, thinly sliced	1	
garlic, minced	2 cloves	
maple syrup	1 tablespoon	15 ml
tart apple, cored and thinly sliced (a Cortland or Northern Spy would be perfect)	1	
sweetened, dried cranberries	1 tablespoon	8 g
apple-smoked bacon	4 slices	
very sharp cheddar cheese, shredded	1 cup	120 g
Parmesan cheese, grated	¼ cup	25 g
salt and pepper	to taste	

1. Preheat the oven to 425°F (220°C) and place a pizza stone on the bottom rack. (See Note on page 33.)

2. In a large saucepan, heat 2 tablespoons (30 ml) of the olive oil over medium-low heat. Add the onion and garlic and sauté until just tender. Add the maple syrup, apple, and cranberries and continue to sauté until the onions, garlic, and apples have caramelized and are golden brown. Set the pan aside.

3. In a clean sauté pan, fry the bacon until crispy. Transfer it to a plate lined with a paper towel and set it aside.

4. Spread the remaining 1 tablespoon (15 ml) olive oil on the dough and sprinkle the pie evenly with the onion-apple mixture. Gently crush the bacon slices and sprinkle them over the top; coat everything evenly with the cheeses. Transfer the pie to the baking stone and bake it for 20 minutes, or until the cheese is melted and the crust is golden brown. Sprinkle with salt and pepper to taste.

Bavarian CALZONES

MAKES 2
CALZONES

MY MOTHER WAS A NOTORIOUS HEALTH NUT. But when she broke from her food strictures, the woman was magnificent. The all-time gastronomic gut bomb was the day we sought sustenance after a five-hour shopping jag in Munich. She spotted a large beer hall and dragged me in. She ordered Camembert and bread. No big whoop, right?

What the waiter brought, however, pleased my Chuck E. Cheese–infused American tummy to no end. The Camembert was an entire saucer-sized round, breaded and *deep fried* to a golden brown. It was hot, molten, and gooey, which immediately rectified the fact that my mother had ordered a fancy French cheese. The bread was crusty and plentiful, and the grub came with a large dish of chunky preserves. The combination was spectacular.

For my calzones, I riff on our culinary adventure and add a few morsels like poached chicken and a little aioli to bring succulence to the proceedings. Accompany this with a lovely glass of German pilsner and give a toast to all the cool moms out there.

FOR THE CRUST		
Pizza Dough (page 33), prepared through step 3	1 batch	
FOR THE FILLING		
small boneless, skinless chicken breasts	2	
chicken stock	4 cups	960 ml
FOR THE AIOLI		
garlic, mashed	1 clove	
egg	1	
lemon juice	1 teaspoon	5 ml
maple syrup	1 tablespoon	15 ml
salt	pinch	5 ml
olive oil	½ cup	120 ml
FOR THE ASSEMBLY		
lingonberry preserves	¼ cup	60 ml
Camembert cheese, sliced	4 ounces	115 g

Procedure for the crust

Follow the recipe for pizza dough on page 33 through step 3. After the dough rises, divide it in half and roll both pieces into rough 8-inch (20-cm) rounds, ⅛ to ¼ inch (3 to 6 mm) thick. Refrigerate them until the filling is ready.

Procedure for the filling

Poach the chicken: Place the chicken breasts in a deep saucepan and pour in the chicken stock. If the stock doesn't cover the chicken completely, add enough water that the chicken is barely submerged. Poach the chicken over medium heat until it's just cooked through, 15 to 20 minutes. Check the center of a breast. If it's still a little pink, that's perfect. You'll continue to cook the chicken in the oven, so a little pink will ensure that the meat will be tender once it's finished. Remove the chicken from the poaching liquid and allow it to cool to room temperature.

Procedure for the aioli

In the bowl of a food processor, combine the garlic, egg, lemon juice, maple syrup, and salt. Pulse the mixture until the garlic is finely chopped and the ingredients are well combined. With the processor running, very slowly add the oil until the aioli is emulsified and thickens.

Assembly

1. Preheat the oven to 350°F (175°C). Line a baking sheet with parchment.

2. Cut the chicken breasts on the bias into ½-inch (12-mm) slices. Place the rounds of pizza dough on the prepared baking sheet. Slather 2 tablespoons (30 ml) of the aioli on each round, leaving 1 inch (2.5 cm) clean around the edges. Divide the lingonberry preserves between the rounds, spreading it on top of the aioli. Arrange the chicken on the rounds, placing it on one half of each round only, and leaving the border clear. Divide the cheese between the two rounds, placing it on top of the chicken.

3. Pull the unfilled half of each round over the chicken and cheese, pinching the edges together and then tucking them under. Bake the calzones for 30 minutes, or until the crust is a deep golden brown.

POTATO
Sausage
PIE

MAKES 1
(10-INCH/25-CM) PIE

IT MIGHT SOUND STRANGE TO YOU THAT POTATOES WOULD MAKE AN APPEARANCE ON A PIZZA PIE, BUT IT'S REALLY QUITE NORMAL . . . IN THE TINY ALSACE REGION OF FRANCE. It's also wonderfully delicious. So why not give it a go? I've added a sprinkling of sausage to get you motivated.

Pizza Dough (page 33), on a peel as directed	1 batch	
olive oil, divided	3 tablespoons	45 ml
heavy cream	½ cup	120 ml
unsalted butter	2 tablespoons	28 g
Parmesan cheese, grated	¼ cup	25 g
large Yukon gold potato, peel left on and very thinly sliced	1	15 g
andouille sausage, casing removed, cut into ½-inch (12-mm) pieces	1 link	
minced fresh rosemary	1 teaspoon	2 g
Gruyère cheese, shredded	1 cup	120 g
salt and pepper	to taste	

1. Preheat the oven to 425°F (220°C) and place a pizza stone on the bottom rack. (See Note on page 33.)

2. In small sauté pan, heat 2 tablespoons (30 ml) of the olive oil over medium-low heat and add the onion and garlic. Sauté until they are soft and caramelized. Set the pan aside.

3. In a shallow pan, heat the cream, butter, and Parmesan until the butter is melted. Add the potatoes and stir to coat them evenly with the cream. Simmer until they are just fork-tender, about 5 minutes.

4. In a clean sauté pan, fry the sausage until it is crispy. Transfer it to a plate lined with a paper towel and set it aside.

5. Spread the remaining 1 tablespoon (15 ml) olive oil over the dough. Sprinkle the rosemary evenly over the round. Gently place the potatoes on the dough in an even layer, being careful not to transfer too much liquid along with them.

6. Sprinkle the sautéed onions and garlic onto the pizza. Gently crumble the sausage over the top and sprinkle that with the Gruyère. Transfer the pie to the baking stone and bake it for 20 minutes, or until the cheese is melted and the crust is golden brown. Sprinkle with salt and pepper to taste.

OKAY, IN ALL FAIRNESS, A *PITHIVIER* IS USUALLY A SWEET PIE (PAGE 103). But I hoped that a little false advertising would get you excited about the whole "chicken-liver-pâté" aspect of this dish. This is scrumptious. If you love a smooth French pâté, you'll adore this tart. Not only is it delicious, but by making the pâté yourself, you'll be getting some seriously great pâté on the cheap. It's delicious (and high in iron), and there's nothing better than puff and pâté!

PÂTÉ
Pithivier

MAKES 1
(12-INCH/30.5-CM) TART

FOR THE CRUST		
Traditional Puff Pastry (page 25)	¼ batch	
FOR THE PÂTÉ		
fresh chicken livers (ask your butcher if you can't find them in the grocery case)	¼ pound	115 g
small sweet yellow onion, thinly sliced	1	
garlic, minced	1 clove	
thyme leaves	½ teaspoon	1 g
cognac	1 tablespoon	15 ml
unsalted butter	½ cup	115 g
salt and pepper	to taste	
FOR THE ASSEMBLY		
firm Bosc pear, peel on, cored and thinly sliced	1	
egg wash (1 egg whisked with 2 tablespoons/30 ml water)		
large-flaked fleur de sel (sea salt), for sprinkling	2 tablespoons	30 g

Procedure for the crust

Divide the dough in half and roll each piece into a 12-inch (30.5-cm) round. Dock one of the rounds and refrigerate both pieces for 20 minutes.

Procedure for the pâté

1. In a very large saucepan, combine the livers, onion, garlic, thyme, and ½ cup (120 ml) water. Simmer for 5 minutes, or until the livers are no longer pink. Take the saucepan from the heat, add the cognac, and let it sit, covered, for 5 minutes.

2. Using a slotted spoon, transfer the contents of the saucepan to the bowl of a food processor; discard the liquid. With the processor running, add the butter, a few small pieces at a time, until a smooth

paste forms. Add salt and pepper to taste. Transfer the pâté to a bowl, cover it with plastic wrap, and refrigerate it until cool.

Assembly

1. Preheat the oven to 375°F (190°C) and line a baking sheet with parchment.

2. Place the docked round of dough on the prepared baking sheet and brush it with the egg wash. Spread the pâté over the dough with a small offset spatula, leaving a 1-inch (2.5-cm) border all around. Cover the pâté with a single layer of the pear slices.

3. Place the second round of dough on top and press down on the edges to seal the rounds together. With a paring knife, score decorative designs on the top of the dough, being careful not to cut all the way through. (I like to etch the guest of honor's initials on top—a little pâté monogram never hurt anyone.) Brush the top of the pastry with egg wash and sprinkle it with sea salt.

4. Bake the pastry for 45 minutes, or until the crust turns a deep golden brown and the edges puff. Cut it into thin wedges and serve it with a lovely Sauternes to start out an evening.

MY MOTHER WAS ALWAYS FULL OF SURPRISES. We'd be eating bulgur wheat and tofu for months, and one day, out of the blue, she'd pull out a grill and heat up some gorgeous cheese and drape it over potatoes. This very thing happened one winter when we were skiing in Wyoming. We had a family house there, and even though we were officially on vacation, our super-healthy eating regimen came with us to the Rockies. And then Helga broke out the yummy stuff when we least expected it.

Raclette is a pungent cheese native to Switzerland, and the dish of the same name is made by heating the cheese and then scraping it onto a plate filled with potatoes, cornichons, and sausage. Me, I like to scrape it onto a round of puff pastry. But I think you could have guessed that.

Raclette
TART

MAKES 1
(4-BY-14-INCH/10-BY-35.5-CM)
RECTANGULAR TART

Traditional Puff Pastry (page 25)	¼ batch	
thick slab bacon, cut into 1-inch (2.5-cm) pieces	4 slices	
unsalted butter	2 tablespoons	28 g
sweet yellow onion, thinly sliced	1	
garlic, minced	2 cloves	
Yukon gold potato, not peeled, thinly sliced (you should be able to see light through the potato, it's so thin)	1	
salt and pepper	to taste	
minced fresh chervil	1 teaspoon	2 g
raclette cheese, finely shredded	1 cup	120 g

1. Preheat the oven to 375°F (190°C) and line a baking sheet with parchment. Roll out the dough into a 6-by-16-inch (15-by-40.5-cm) rectangle. Dock the dough and transfer it to the prepared baking sheet. Refrigerate it for 20 minutes.

2. In a large skillet, render the bacon pieces until they are brown and slightly crispy. With a slotted spoon, transfer them to a plate lined with a paper towel. In the same skillet, melt the butter with the leftover bacon fat and sauté the onion and garlic until the pieces are soft and slightly golden. Set the pan aside to cool.

3. Take a very sharp paring knife and gently score a line ½ inch (12 mm) from the edge of the rectangle, all around. Don't cut all the way through, but just enough that you can easily fold the edges of the dough up to create walls. Pinch the edges of the dough to keep the walls up.

4. Layer the slices of potato evenly on top of the dough and then season with salt and pepper and sprinkle with chervil. Top the potatoes with the caramelized onions and garlic, evenly distribute the bacon pieces on top of the onions, and finish by layering the cheese over all.

5. Bake the tart for 25 to 30 minutes, or until the edges are deep golden brown and the cheese is bubbling.

A NOTE FROM THE SWEETIE PIE

Every cell in my being revolts at the words *hot-water crust*. And yet, it's the stuff of "noble pies." Noble pies are "raised pies," pastries that were served to gentry only. The pies required a sturdy crust because they were often baked in very tall embossed tins, which when removed left lovely patterns on the pastry. If the pastry wasn't sturdy, it wouldn't stay upright and wouldn't take the pattern. Honestly, a hot-water crust isn't half bad. If you happen to lay your hands on an antique pie tin that's hinged and embossed and probably laced with lead and you're brave enough to use it, make a hot-water crust to achieve the best results.

Here's what you do: Take 1 pound (455 g) flour, 1 teaspoon (6 g) salt, and 1 tablespoon (11 g) sugar and whisk them in a large bowl. Make a well in the flour mixture and crack an egg into it. Whisk everything together. It will be chunky. In the meantime, in a large saucepan, combine 1 cup (240 ml) water, ¼ pound (115 g) butter, and ¼ pound (115 g) lard (if you're going to go noble, go lard). Bring the mixture to a boil and then pour it into the mixing bowl with the flour and egg, stirring all the while with a fork to ensure that you don't scramble the egg. Turn the dough out onto a flour-dusted work surface and knead it until it is smooth and no egg streaks remain. Use it immediately! The stuff hardens (like homemade Play-Doh) as it cools. It's a little wet and strange to work with, but it's an adventure!

CHAPTER

4

Pie It

FORWARD!

Now that we know what's possible, let's accomplish the impossible. Let's make masterpieces out of the tastiest components on earth. Let's make pie into an art form. Taking the skills you've learned, think outside the pie plate and stack your crusts and fillings into layers! Ring them with gorgeous edible sides! Make those ready-to-wear pies into (edible) haute couture.

For a video demonstration of some of the techniques featured in this chapter, go to www.pieitforwardcookbook.com.

Strawberry LOVE PIE

MAKES 1
(10-INCH/25-CM) PIE

THE STRAWBERRY LOVE PIE WAS ONE OF THE ALL-TIME FAVORITE TREATS AT GESINE CONFECTIONARY. The simple pairing of strawberries at their peak with creamy vanilla is the very essence of summer. Layer those two into crisp and buttery puff pastry, and your mouth will sing! But wrap the glorious whole in beautiful décor sides made with joconde sponge, and there's no other pie that screams "love!" like this one.

My version of joconde is a spongier sponge recipe. The options for joconde in this application are either a very thin and elegant joconde that easily becomes brittle or a thicker and easier-to-bend joconde. I'm for easier-to-bend anytime. The decorative element comes from writing or creating patterns with a tuille paste first and then covering the décor with a thin layer of the joconde cake batter.

FOR THE TUILLE BATTER		
unsalted butter, softened	½ cup	115 g
confectioners' sugar, sifted	½ cup, plus 1 tablespoon	50 g, plus 5 g
egg whites	¼ cup	60 ml
sifted bread flour	5 tablespoons	38 g
food coloring or cocoa powder, for coloring		
FOR THE JOCONDE SPONGE		
almond flour (or sliced, blanched almonds)	3 ounces	85 g
confectioners' sugar	1 cup	100 g
all-purpose flour	¼ cup	30 g
salt	½ teaspoon	3 g
eggs	3	
egg yolk	1	
egg whites	2	
granulated sugar	3 tablespoons	30 g
unsalted butter, melted	1 tablespoon	14 g
FOR THE CRUST		
Traditional Puff Pastry (page 25)	½ batch	
FOR THE FILLINGS		
strawberries, hulled and cut in half	2 pints	680 g
granulated sugar, divided	1 cup	200 g
zest and juice of 1 lemon		
minced fresh basil	1 teaspoon	2 g

Ingredients continued on next page

egg yolks	6	
cornstarch	¼ cup	32 g
salt	pinch	
heavy cream, divided	2 cups	480 ml
milk	1 cup	240 ml
mascarpone cheese	¾ cup	175 g
vanilla bean paste	1 tablespoon	15 ml
FOR THE ASSEMBLY		
heavy cream	2 cups	480 ml
confectioners' sugar	¼ cup	25 g
strawberries	1 pint	340 g

Procedure for the tuille

1. In the bowl of a stand mixer fitted with the paddle attachment, make the tuille batter by creaming the butter and confectioners' sugar until well combined but not fluffy. Slowly add the egg whites, scraping the bowl occasionally. You'll notice that the paste starts to break apart; this is normal. Add the flour but don't overmix; you want a smooth paste. Add a few drops of food coloring (or, if you want brown, a few tablespoons of cocoa powder), mixing one last time to distribute the color.

2. Make a guide for the decorations of the side of your pie: Take two pieces of parchment the size of a half sheet pan, fold each in half lengthwise, and use the fold as a guide to draw a dividing line with a permanent marker. You should be left with two "zones" on each piece of parchment, each measuring roughly 18 by 7½ inches. Using the marker, write "LOVE" continuously down the center of each zone, leaving a few inches between words so each "LOVE" stands alone. I write the letters at least 4 inches tall. Continue writing your message and making other designs (like small hearts) on your parchment and place it, face side down, under a nonstick silicone baking mat on a sheet pan. (When making joconde décor sides, always pipe your batter directly onto a nonstick baking mat, not onto parchment; the batter tends to stick to everything but baking mats.) Using the words and shapes on the parchment as your guide, trace the letters and shapes onto the baking mat with the tuille batter. (The reason you flipped the parchment around and are now writing the words backwards is that when you remove the sides to wrap around the cake, the side facing up on the pan is the side that will attach to the cake.)

3. When you have written all of your messages and made all the decorative elements you want with the batter, freeze them for at least 1 hour, until they're rock hard.

4. Remove the parchment stencil from underneath the baking mat and discard.

Procedure for the joconde sponge

1. In the bowl of a food processor, combine the almond flour and confectioners' sugar. Process for a few minutes, until you have a very fine mixture (finer than sand). Add the all-purpose flour, salt, eggs, and egg yolk and process until everything is completely incorporated.

2. Place the egg whites in the very clean bowl of a stand mixer fitted with the whisk attachment and beat them until they're frothy. Slowly add the granulated sugar and beat just until you have stiff peaks.

3. Pour the sugar-almond mixture into the bowl with the egg whites and start folding the two together with a large rubber spatula. You want to get major air bubbles out of the mixture but maintain an airy texture. Once you've incorporated the two, fold in the melted butter and make sure it is evenly distributed into the batter.

4. Preheat the oven to 400°F (205°C).

5. Make sure your tuille patterns are frozen solid, then divide the joconde mixture between the two sheet pans, on top of the tuille. Tilt the pan here and there to let the joconde spread, then work very gently with a small offset spatula to make it even, taking care not to smear the underlying writing or decorations.

6. Immediately transfer the pans to the oven and bake them for 3 to 5 minutes. As I'm paranoid, I turn the sheet pans a few times during baking. When it's done, the batter should spring back when touched and may have a little browning. Make sure there's no hint of wetness. Set aside to cool completely.

Procedure for the crust

1. Reduce the oven temperature to 350°F (175°C).

2. Divide the dough into quarters and roll each piece into a rough 11-inch (28-cm) round. Allow the dough rounds to rest in the refrigerator for at least 20 minutes.

3. Using a sharp knife, trim each round into a very neat 10-inch (25-cm) circle. Transfer the rounds to parchment-lined baking sheets. (Keep in mind that in the next step you'll need an extra baking sheet for every baking sheet you fill with dough rounds now—so you'll have to work in batches if you don't have enough oven space or baking sheets. If you aren't baking all the pieces at once, refrigerate the dough that's waiting in line.)

4. Bake each round for 10 minutes. At that point you'll notice that the puff is really starting to—well, puff. Place a piece of parchment on top of the puffing round and set another (empty) baking sheet on top of the parchment to weight the puff down a bit. Bake the weighted rounds for 10 minutes more, then remove the empty pan and bake for an additional 5 minutes, or until the puff is cooked through. Repeat as necessary until you have a total of 4 rounds. Set the rounds aside to cool completely.

Procedure for the fillings

1. In a large bowl, stir together the strawberries, ½ cup (100 g) of the sugar, the lemon zest and juice, and the basil. Let the berries macerate for at least 20 minutes, until the sugar has dissolved and the strawberries have released some of their liquid.

2. In the bowl of a stand mixer fitted with the whisk attachment, beat together the remaining sugar, the egg yolks, cornstarch, and salt until smooth and fluffy. Meanwhile, in a large, heavy saucepan, simmer together 1 cup (240 ml) of the cream and the milk.

3. With the mixer set on medium speed, carefully pour the hot milk mixture down the side of the bowl and into the egg yolks. Beat until the mixture is combined.

4. Transfer the mixture back into the saucepan and whisk it over medium-high heat until it thickens to the consistency of mayonnaise. Transfer the pastry cream to a bowl and cover the top with plastic wrap laid directly on the surface to prevent a skin from forming. Refrigerate until cool.

5. In the bowl of a stand mixer fitted with the whisk attachment, beat the remaining 1 cup (240 ml) cream, the mascarpone, and the vanilla until stiff peaks form.

6. Remove the pastry cream from the refrigerator and stir with a wooden spoon to loosen it. Add one-third of the whipped-cream mixture and stir vigorously until the mixture is smooth. Using a large rubber spatula, gently fold the remaining whipped cream into the pastry cream until no white streaks remain.

Assembly

1. Place a 10-inch (25-cm) cake ring or springform pan on a parchment-lined baking sheet. Gently push a puff pastry round into the ring until it hits the bottom.

2. Distribute one-third of the macerated strawberries evenly over the pastry round. Sprinkle a few tablespoons of the juice over the strawberries. Layer one-quarter of the lightened pastry cream on top of the strawberries, spreading it evenly with a small offset spatula. Top with the second round of pastry. Continue this way until you have placed the last layer of pastry on top. Refrigerate the remaining one-quarter of the lightened pastry cream. Freeze the assembled pie for at least 2 hours or overnight, until set.

3. Remove the cake ring by gently heating the sides with a heat gun or blow dryer. With an offset spatula, spread a very thin layer of the remaining pastry cream onto the sides of the pie, creating a scratch coat. You should still be able to see the sides of the pastry rounds. (This layer serves to even out the exterior of the pie and to create an adhesive for the joconde sides.)

4. Cut the joconde sheets in half, trimming any uneven edges. Take the first half and very carefully affix one end to the side of the pie, then gently turn the pie as you continue to wrap the joconde around it. Take the second piece and continue where you left off, trimming any extra. Wrap the pie in plastic wrap and refrigerate it for 30 minutes to set.

5. Finally, in the bowl of a stand mixer fitted with the whisk attachment, whip the cream and confectioners' sugar to stiff peaks. Transfer the whipped cream to a large piping bag fitted with a large star tip. Pipe rosettes over the entire top of the cake and place the fresh strawberries around the perimeter. Serve immediately.

The
BEE
STING

MAKES 8
(2 ½-INCH/6-CM) PIES

NOTE

To make tuille patterns, like stripes, professional pastry chefs use expensive tools available only to the trade. But I've found that wide-toothed icing scrapers work just as well. Or go to the paint department at your hardware store: At The Home Depot I found a four-piece specialty-paint-finish tool set to make sponging effects, stripes, and faux wood grain. The striping comb was a smaller version of the $250 pastry tool that does exactly the same thing.

IT'S HARD TO NOT FALL IN LOVE WITH THIS CAKE, WITH ITS JAUNTY STRIPED SIDES AND THOSE LOVELY LITTLE BEES NESTLED IN THE GANACHE. But then I find it hard to resist most things that combine almond, chocolate, and honey.

FOR THE TUILLE		
tuille batter (see page 226), made with 2 tablespoons/10 g dark cocoa powder for coloring	1 batch	
FOR THE JOCONDE SPONGE		
joconde sponge (see page 226)	1 batch	
FOR THE CRUST		
Traditional Puff Pastry (page 25), Cocoa option	½ batch	
FOR THE FILLING		
bittersweet chocolate, finely chopped	1 pound	455 g
heavy cream	1½ cups	360 ml
egg yolks	6	
sugar	¼ cup	50 g
almond extract	1 tablespoon	15 ml
salt	pinch	
honey (preferably local)	⅓ cup	75 ml
FOR THE GANACHE		
bittersweet chocolate, finey chopped	8 ounces	226g
heavy cream	¾ cup	177ml
corn syrup	1 tablespoon	15 ml
salt	pinch	
FOR THE ASSEMBLY		
marzipan	4 ounces	115 g
bittersweet chocolate	4 ounces	115 g
blanched almond slices (not slivers)	1 cup	90 g
SPECIAL EQUIPMENT		
silicone painting comb (see Note)		

For the tuille

1. Follow the procedure for making tuille paste described in step 1 on page 228. Tint the batter with cocoa powder.

2. Using an offset spatula, spread the tuille batter in a very thin, even layer across a nonstick silicone baking mat. Drag a painting comb across the parchment lengthwise. Scrape the extra batter off the comb and make additional stripes below the first set as needed. Freeze the tuille until it's rock hard, at least 1 hour.

Procedure for the joconde sponge

Follow the procedure on page 229 for making joconde sponge, pouring it over the tuille decorations, and baking the sponge.

Procedure for the crust

1. Reduce the oven temperature to 350°F (175°C).

2. Divide the dough in half. Roll each piece into a rough rectangle approximately the size of a half sheet pan (12 by 16 inches/30.5 by 40.5 cm). Transfer each rectangle to a parchment-lined baking sheet and allow the dough to rest for 20 minutes in the refrigerator. (Keep in mind that in the next step you'll need an extra baking sheet for every baking sheet you fill with dough now—so you'll have to work in batches if you don't have enough oven space or baking sheets. If you aren't baking all the pieces at once, refrigerate the dough that's waiting in line.)

3. Bake the dough for 10 minutes, or until the pastry starts to puff. Place a piece of parchment on top of the pastry and then carefully place an empty baking sheet on top of the parchment to gently weight down the pastry. (You don't want to smoosh the puff, just tame it a little with an even distribution of weight.) Bake for 10 minutes more. Remove the empty baking sheet and continue baking until the pastry is baked through, about 10 minutes. Set aside to cool completely.

4. Take a cake ring, 2½ inches (6 cm) wide by 3 inches (7.5 cm) high, and use it to cut 24 rounds from the two pieces of puff pastry. Place 8 of the rounds on a parchment-lined sheet pan. Place a cake ring, 2½ inches (6 cm) wide by 3 inches (7.5 cm) tall, over each of the 8 rounds, so a piece of pastry is nestled at the bottom of each ring— these are the bottom layers of the "pie cakes." Set aside. Reserve the remaining 16 rounds.

Procedure for the filling

1. Place the chocolate in a large metal bowl and place the bowl over a large pot of simmering water. Stir the chocolate until it's completely melted, being careful not to let it scorch or burn. Set the chocolate aside to cool, but don't let it harden.

2. In the bowl of a stand mixer fitted with the whisk attachment, whip the cream to stiff peaks. Transfer the whipped cream to a bowl and set it aside. In the same bowl of the stand mixer, whip the egg yolks, sugar, almond extract, and salt until light and aerated.

3. Pour the honey into a small saucepan and heat it over low heat until it starts to gently boil. With the mixer still running, carefully pour the honey down the side of the bowl into the egg-yolk mixture. Turn the mixer speed to high and beat until the mixture has cooled.

4. Fold in the melted chocolate and then quickly fold in the whipped cream. Take care that each element is similar in temperature; otherwise, your chocolate can seize, and you'll end up with little chunks of hard chocolate in your filling. (This is still tasty but not ideal.)

5. Transfer the filling to a large pastry bag fitted with a large open tip. Pipe an even layer of filling (about 1 inch/2.5 cm thick) inside each of the 8 cake rings, right on top of the round of pastry. Place a reserved round of pastry on top of the first layer of filling in each cake ring. Press gently. The fit is very snug and the puff is delicate, but you want the second layer of pastry to sit on top of the filling. (I sometimes trim the edges of the remaining rounds of pastry very carefully, to make inserting them into the rings easier; if you choose to do this, be careful to cut as evenly as possible.) Pipe another 1-inch (2.5-cm) layer of filling onto the second round of pastry inside each ring. Top with the last 8 rounds, pressing gently. If the last round of pastry doesn't reach the top of the ring, divide the remaining filling evenly among the rings and, using a small offset spatula, gently scrape the top to make it even.

6. Freeze the pies until set, about 2 hours.

Procedure for the ganache

1. Place the chocolate in a mixing bowl. Set aside. In a heavy saucepan over medium-high heat, stir the cream, butter, corn syrup, and salt until the butter has completely melted and the mixture comes to a low simmer. Pour the cream mixture over the chocolate and allow to sit for a few minutes, undisturbed, to allow the chocolate to melt. Then whisk the mixture until emulsified and smooth.

2. Remove the pies from the freezer and place a heaping tablespoon of ganache on top of each pie. Smooth with an offset spatula. Return the pies back to the freezer for 10 minutes to allow the ganache to set.

Assembling the Bees

1. Remove the pies from the cake rings by placing each pie on top of a tall container that's slightly narrower than the pie itself (I use a spice bottle). Gently heat the sides of the ring with a heat gun or blow dryer and

carefully tug the ring down so it falls away from the pie. Continue with the remaining pies.

2. Cut the décor sides: Wrap a piece of kitchen twine around the circumference of the pie (it should be around 8¾ inches/22 cm, but it's always safer to take your own measurement) and cut the twine to the exact circumference. This is your joconde-side measurement.

3. Before you take the décor sides out of the sheet pan, gently dust the joconde with confectioners' sugar. Trim the outer edges of the cake with a thin paring knife. Place a piece of parchment over the cake; then place a sheet pan over the parchment and flip the cake over. Carefully remove the top sheet pan and then very gently remove the baking mat. Cut 8 pieces of joconde to match the measurement you made with the twine.

4. Using a small offset spatula, smooth a very thin layer of ganache around each little pie to create an adhesive for the joconde. Gently wrap a joconde strip around the pie, pressing gently, and wrap with a piece of plastic wrap. Refrigerate for 20 minutes to allow the joconde strip to adhere properly.

5. Pinch dime-size pieces of marzipan from the small loaf. Roll the pieces in your hand to make an oval shape about ½ inch (6 mm) in length. Continue making ovals until you have a total of 8.

6. Take the pies from the fridge and place the ovals of marzipan on top of each pie.

7. In a microwave-safe bowl, melt the chocolate in 30-second bursts until it is melted. Allow the chocolate to cool slightly, but make sure it remains soft. Transfer it to a small piping bag fitted with a small open pastry tip. Pipe strips of chocolate along the backs of the marzipan ovals. For wings, take two slices of almond and place one on either side of each bee, using a touch of melted chocolate at the bottom as glue. At the head of the bee, pipe two little dots of chocolate for eyes.

8. Serve immediately.

THIS ISN'T A SAD PIE. It's a pie full of sunshiny yellow lemon and brilliant blue blueberries. It's the happiest pie on earth, if you can get a slice. With its buttery, crunchy puff layered with silken lemon curd, soft whipped cream, and abundant fresh blueberries, this is a bright light on any dessert table.

LEMON
Blues

MAKES 1
(10-INCH/25-CM) PIE

FOR THE CRUST		
Traditional Puff Pastry (page 25)	½ batch	
FOR THE CURD FILLING		
lemon juice, divided	1 cup plus 2 tablespoons	240 ml plus 30 ml
granulated sugar	2 cups	400 g
egg yolks	14	
unflavored gelatin	1 teaspoon	2.5 g
unsalted butter	2 tablespoons	28 g
FOR THE CREAM FILLING		
heavy cream	2 cups	480 ml
mascarpone cheese	½ cup	115 g
confectioners' sugar	½ cup	50 g
lemon extract	1 teaspoon	5 ml
FOR THE ASSEMBLY		
fresh blueberries, picked over and destemmed	2 pints	680 g
white chocolate	1 pound	455 g
SPECIAL EQUIPMENT		
transfer sheets, in the pattern of your choice	2	

Procedure for the crust

1. Preheat the oven to 350°F (175°C). Divide the dough into quarters and roll each piece into a rough 11-inch (28-cm) round. Allow the rounds to rest in the refrigerator for at least 20 minutes.

2. Using a sharp knife, trim each round into a very neat 10-inch (25-cm) circle. Transfer the rounds to parchment-lined baking sheets. (Keep in mind that in the next step you'll need an extra baking sheet for every baking sheet you fill with dough now—so you'll have to work in batches if you don't have enough oven space or baking sheets. If you aren't baking all the pieces at once, refrigerate the dough that's waiting in line.)

3. Bake each round for 10 minutes. At that point you'll notice that the puff is really starting to—well, puff. Place a piece of parchment on top of the puffing round and set another (empty) baking sheet on top of the parchment to weight the puff down a bit. Continue baking the weighted rounds for 10 minutes more, then remove the empty pan and bake for an additional 5 minutes, or until the puff is cooked through. Set the rounds aside to cool completely.

Procedure for the curd filling

1. In a heatproof metal bowl, combine 1 cup (240 ml) of the lemon juice, the granulated sugar, and the egg yolks. In a separate bowl, sprinkle the gelatin on top of the remaining 2 tablespoons (30 ml) lemon juice until it blooms and looks soggy. Set it aside.

2. Place the heatproof bowl over a pot of simmering water and whisk until the lemon mixture has thickened enough that it ribbons when you pull out the whisk. Remove the bowl from the heat. Immediately add the gelatin and whisk until it is completely melted. Add the butter and whisk until it is fully incorporated.

3. Transfer the curd to a large bowl and cover with plastic wrap laid directly on the surface to prevent a skin from forming. Refrigerate the curd until cool, at least 2 hours.

Procedure for the cream filling

In the bowl of a stand mixer fitted with the whisk attachment, whip together the cream, mascarpone, confectioners' sugar, lemon extract, and 2 tablespoons (30 ml) of the lemon curd until stiff peaks form.

Assembly

1. Place a 10-inch (25-cm) cake ring or springform pan on a parchment-lined baking sheet. Gently push a pastry round to the bottom of the ring or pan.

2. Spoon one-quarter of the remaining curd onto the pastry and spread it evenly with a small offset spatula. Sprinkle it with 1 cup (170 g) fresh blueberries. Top the blueberries with one-third of the cream mixture. Top with another round of pastry. Build two more pie layers, covering each with curd, blueberries, and cream. Place the last round on top of the cream. Wrap the cake in plastic wrap and freeze it for at least 2 hours or overnight, until set. Refrigerate the remaining lemon curd and blueberries, reserving them for finishing the pie.

3. Trim the sides of the chocolate transfer sheets to remove any extraneous bits that aren't an actual part of the pattern (there's empty space and often some manufacturer's printing along the sides).

4. Measure the outside circumference of the pie using a piece of kitchen twine. Cut the twine to the measurement of the pie, plus ½ inch (12 mm) extra. Measure the height of the pie with a ruler and note the measurement.

5. Cut each transfer sheet in half lengthwise. Using the height measurement of the pie and a ruler, trim each piece lengthwise as neatly as possible so you have 2 chocolate strips the same height as the cake. It's easiest to use an X-Acto knife or a razor blade for the trimming; scissors require you to handle the sheet too much, which tends to cause the chocolate to rub off.

6. Line a work surface with parchment, then place the transfer-sheet strips on it, chocolate side down and shiny side up. Line the strips up next to each other and tape them together so you form a continuous piece. Using the piece of twine as a guide, cut the attached strips to the same length as the circumference of the cake. Flip the transfer sheet over so the shiny side is down and the textured side is up.

7. Temper the white chocolate (see Note). Spread the white chocolate onto the transfer sheets and apply them to the sides of the pie. Do not peel away the plastic sheeting from the transfer sheets yet.

8. Layer the top of the pie with the remaining lemon curd and top it with a layer of blueberries. Remove the plastic sheeting from the transfer sheets and serve.

If you've eaten a fresh, high-quality bar of chocolate, you've experienced chocolate in perfect temper. That means it's shiny and snaps when you break it. Sometimes, chocolate is stored in warm conditions, melts a bit, and then cools again. When you unwrap that particular bar of chocolate, you may notice white streaking that looks almost like mold. It's not. What you are seeing is chocolate out of temper. The consistency is also different; you won't get that satisfying snap when you break it apart.

Unless you get your chocolate to the perfect temper and temperature, the transfer design won't adhere when you spread it onto a transfer sheet. This is why people often prefer to use a chocolate candy coating that adheres to the chocolate transfer easily, as you need only melt and spread a thin layer without the technicalities of tempering. (Wilton is the most available brand.) However, candy coatings contain palm oils and paraffin, and the taste, compared to a high-quality tempered chocolate, is never quite the same. I recommend tempering for that reason but recognize the ease and the significant time (and monetary) difference of using widely available chocolate candy coatings instead.

You must use a high-quality chocolate for tempering; the stuff you buy at the checkout at the grocery ain't gonna cut it—it doesn't have the cocoa-butter content needed. Buy a high-quality chocolate like Callebaut, Lindt, or Valrhona.

Getting chocolate to the right temperature and into temper requires a nice amount of chocolate, and you rarely use the entire amount that you temper. You can always use the leftover chocolate for something else later.

To Temper Chocolate

1. Have a digital, instant-read thermometer ready. Chop the required amount of your high-quality chocolate into very small pieces, making sure to keep the pieces uniform so they melt evenly.

2. Transfer two-thirds of the chocolate to a microwave-safe bowl. Heat the chocolate at 50% power in 30-second increments, stirring in between blasts with a rubber spatula. Continue zapping until the chocolate is melted and the temperature reads 110°F (43°C). Take your time. Don't burn the chocolate, and don't go over temperature.

3. Stir in one-third of the remaining unmelted chocolate. Gently stir until the chocolate is evenly distributed into the melted chocolate. Wait about 10 minutes and take the chocolate's temperature. It should be between 95°F and 100°F (35°C and 38°C).

4. Add another one-third of the unmelted chocolate, stir gently, and allow the mixture to rest for a few minutes. Dark chocolate is in temper when its temperature is between 90°F and 93°F (32°C and 34°C); white chocolate's is between 86°F and 90°F (30°C and 32°C). Stir gently and take the temperature of the chocolate again. If it's still too high, add the remaining bits of chocolate, stir, rest for a minute, and take the temperature. Continue stirring, resting, and checking the thermometer until the chocolate reaches temperature.

5. To test the tempering, dip the back of a spoon in the chocolate and let it sit. If after 5 minutes it's still shiny and has hardened a bit, you're safe. If it's still very wet and streaky, you're not yet in temper.

COCOA PUFF

MAKES 1
(10-INCH/25-CM) PIE

CHOCOLATE AND PEANUT BUTTER. Now, there's a combination that is delicious but rarely beautiful. That's not the case here! For a dessert that makes for a gleeful celebration for children and adults alike, whip up this glorious masterpiece and get ready for a treat.

FOR THE CRUST		
Traditional Puff Pastry (page 25), Chocolate option	½ batch	
FOR THE FILLING		
heavy cream	2 cups	480 ml
creamy peanut butter	2 cups	510 g
cream cheese	1 pound (two 8-ounce packages)	455 g
confectioners' sugar	1½ cups	150 g
vanilla bean paste	1 tablespoon	15 ml
salt	½ teaspoon	3 g
FOR THE GANACHE		
bittersweet chocolate, finely chopped	1 pound	455 g
heavy cream	1½ cups	360 ml
unsalted butter	2 tablespoons	28 g
FOR THE ASSEMBLY		
roasted, salted peanuts	2 cups	300 g
bittersweet chocolate	2 pounds	910 g
SPECIAL EQUIPMENT		
chocolate transfer sheets, in the pattern of your choice	2	

Procedure for the crust

Follow the instructions on page 237 for cutting and baking 4 (10-inch/25-cm) flattened rounds of puff pastry (Lemon Blues recipe, procedure for the crust). Set the rounds aside to cool.

Procedure for the filling

1. In the bowl of a stand mixer fitted with the whisk attachment, beat the cream to very stiff peaks. Transfer the whipped cream to a large bowl and refrigerate it.

2. Fit the mixer with the paddle attachment and, in the same bowl, beat together the peanut butter, cream cheese, confectioners' sugar, vanilla, and salt until smooth and creamy.

3. Add one-third of the whipped cream to the peanut-butter mixture and beat until well combined. Add the remaining whipped cream and gently fold it into the mixture with a large rubber spatula until no streaks remain. Refrigerate the filling.

Procedure for the ganache

Place the chocolate in a heatproof mixing bowl. In a heavy saucepan over medium heat, bring the cream and butter to a simmer. Pour this mixture over the chocolate and let it sit undisturbed for a few minutes. Once the chocolate has melted, whisk the mixture until smooth. Allow the ganache to cool slightly.

Assembly

1. Use a 10-inch (25-cm) cake ring or springform pan as a mold for building the pie. Place the ring or pan on a parchment-lined baking sheet. Gently place a round of puff pastry inside, nudging it all the way down to the bottom.

2. Spread ¼ cup (60 ml) of the ganache evenly over the puff pastry and then sprinkle ⅓ cup (50 g) of the peanuts over the ganache. Allow the ganache to set in the refrigerator or freezer for 5 minutes.

3. Spread ⅓ of the peanut-butter mixture on top of the ganache layer, smooth it with a small offset spatula, and top it with another round of puff pastry.

4. Repeat steps 2 and 3, continuing with the puff, ganache, peanuts, chill time, and peanut-butter mixture until you've put the last piece of puff on the pie. Do not spread any ganache on this last round. Instead, carefully cover the whole pie with plastic wrap and freeze it for at least 2 hours, or overnight. Refrigerate the remaining ganache; you'll use it to finish the pie.

5. When you're ready, remove the pie from the freezer. Using a blow dryer or a heat gun, warm the sides of the cake ring or pan and very gently remove it. Transfer the pie to a serving plate. Allow it to rest in the refrigerator while you prepare the transfer sheets.

6. Trim the sides of the chocolate transfer sheets to remove any extraneous bits that aren't an actual part of the pattern (there's empty space and often some manufacturer's printing along the sides).

7. Measure the outside circumference of the pie using a piece of kitchen twine. Cut the twine to the measurement of the pie, plus ½ inch (12 mm) extra. Measure the height of the pie with a ruler and note the measurement.

8. Cut each transfer sheet in half lengthwise. Using the height measurement of the pie and a ruler, trim each piece lengthwise as neatly as possible so you have 2 chocolate strips the same height as the cake. It's easiest to use an X-Acto knife or a razor blade for the trimming; scissors require you to handle the sheet too much, which tends to cause the chocolate to rub off.

9. Line a work surface with parchment, then place the transfer-sheet strips on it, chocolate side down and shiny side up. Line the strips up next to each other and tape them together so you form a continuous piece. Using the piece of twine as a guide, cut the attached strips to the same length as the circumference of the cake. Flip the transfer sheet over so the shiny side is down and the textured side is up.

10. Temper the bittersweet chocolate by following the directions on page 241.

11. Spoon a small amount of the tempered chocolate down the middle of your transfer-sheet strip. Using a small offset spatula, gently spread the chocolate in a *very* thin layer over the entire sheet. Make sure to cover the edges well; you'll end up spreading the chocolate over the sides of the transfer, but don't worry—you'll trim away the extra.

12. Allow the chocolate to set for 3 minutes, but do not let it harden. It needs to remain malleable.

13. Using a sharp paring knife, trim around the sides of the transfer sheet where the chocolate has overlapped. Carefully pick up the transfer sheet, placing one end against the side of the cake, shiny side out, chocolate side touching the cake. Slowly wrap the cake in the sheet,

gently rubbing the sides of the transfer to smooth the sheet and ensure that it adheres to the pie. Once you have completely wrapped the pie, tape the two ends of the transfer sheet to each other (they should meet). Refrigerate it to allow the chocolate to set completely, at least 20 minutes.

14. Gently rewarm the remaining ganache so that it's spreadable. Spoon just enough ganache over the top of the pie to coat it evenly. Use an offset spatula to smooth the ganache. Refrigerate the pie for 10 minutes, or until the ganache is set.

15. Remove the tape and very carefully peel away the plastic sheeting from the transfer sides to reveal the pattern. To serve, dip a very sharp serrated knife in scalding-hot water, dry the knife, and cut a slice. Continue dipping the knife in hot water before each cut you make in the cake.

the *the* INDEX

page references in italic refer
to illustrations